IN DEFENSE
OF
MARTIN LUTHER

IN DEFENSE

OF

MARTIN LUTHER

ESSAYS BY

JOHN WARWICK MONTGOMERY

NORTHWESTERN PUBLISHING HOUSE
MILWAUKEE, WISCONSIN

To

Prof. Dr. Wilhelm Oesch
Lutherische Theologische Hochschule
Oberursel, Germany

CONTENTS

FOREWORD

"The Luther research movement, which took its origin in recent years largely from Karl Holl's work, and which has produced a 'veritable Luther-renaissance' in our understanding of the reformer, has been based on two cardinal principles: first, Luther must be allowed to speak for himself, not through the mouths of later interpreters, whether friend or foe; and second, the touchstone in Luther's interpretation must be the reformer's central convictions, not his occasional remarks. . . ."

These words are a clue to the understanding of Dr. Martin Luther as presented in this collection of essays by Dr. John Warwick Montgomery. Without a doubt they are also the key to Dr. Montgomery's consistent defense not only of Luther, but of Lutheran doctrine today. A study of these essays should be worthwhile for all who would absorb Luther's spirit.

It is with this in mind that the *Commission on Christian Literature* of the Wisconsin Evangelical Lutheran Synod authorized the publication of this volume by the Northwestern Publishing House.

H. WICKE

ACKNOWLEDGMENTS

Several American and European publications have carried the essays which, now in revised form, constitute this book. Here follows a complete list of previously authorized appearances of these essays in print:

"95 Theses Then and Now": *Christianity Today*. October 27, 1967 (under the title: "95 Theses for the 450th Anniversary of the Reformation"), Copyright 1967 [1962] by *Christianity Today*, reprinted by permission; in German translation, alongside Luther's original theses, as a pamphlet titled, *Reformation — einst und jetzt* (Bremen: Verlag Stelten, 1967; hrsg. im Auftrag der Deutschen Geschäftsstelle der Lutherischen Stunde); Luther's Theses, *Luther's Ninety-Five Theses* (originally from the *Lutheran Cyclopedia*), Concordia Publishing House, St. Louis, Missouri, used by permission.

"Luther's Hermeneutic vs. the New Hermeneutic": *Aspects of Biblical Hermeneutics, Confessional Principles and Practical Applications — CTM Occasional Papers No. 1 — c 1966* (under the title: "Lutheran Hermeneutics and Hermeneutics Today"), Concordia Publishing House, St. Louis, Missouri, used by permission; *Lutherischer Rundblick*, XV/1 [1967] (in German); as a chapter in the author's *Crisis in Lutheran Theology*, Vol. I (Grand Rapids, Michigan: Baker Book House, 1967); *Positions Luthériennes*, Avril, 1968 (in French).

"Luther and Science": *Transactions of the Royal Society of Canada*, 4th ser., I [1963], 251-70, (under the title: "Cross, Constellation, and Crucible: Lutheran Astrology and Alchemy in the Age of the Reformation"), reprinted by permission of the Royal Society of Canada; *Ambix, the Journal of the Society for the Study of Alchemy and Early Chemistry*, June, 1963; *Revue d'Histoire et de Philosophie Religieuses*, 1966 (in French).

"Luther, Libraries, and Learning": *The Library Quarterly* [University of Chicago Press], Vol. XXXII, No. 2, [April, 1962] (under the title: "Luther and Libraries"), copyright by The University of Chicago Press 1962, used by permission.

"Shirer's Re-Hitlerizing of Luther": *The Christian Century*, December 12, 1962; copyright 1962 Christian Century Foundation, reprinted by permission.

"A Day in East German Luther Country": *Christian Herald*, June 1965 (in abbreviated form); *Evangelize* [Lutheran Evangelistic Movement, Minneapolis], October and November, 1967 (with corrigendum in the January, 1968, issue), used by permission.

"Luther and the Missionary Challenge": *Evangelical Missions Quarterly*, Vol. 3, No. 4 [Summer 1967] (under the title: "Luther and Missions"), used by permission.

LUTHER CARICATURED AS A SEVEN-HEADED MONSTER

INTRODUCTION

To defend Martin Luther — whose courage in the face of overwhelming religious and secular attack has become a byword in world history — may well seem a superfluous if not presumptive task. One is reminded of the exchange between an eager young man and the great 19th century evangelist Charles Finney. Young man: "Mr. Finney, how can I defend the Bible?" Finney: "How would you defend a lion? Let it out of its cage and it will defend itself!"

In a very real sense, Finney's reply is applicable to Luther. Since the monumental and as yet uncompleted labor of the Weimarer Ausgabe began in 1888 and the so-called Luther-research movement commenced in the labors of Karl Holl at Tübingen, the Reformer has been "let out of the cage" of secondary and tertiary interpretations to speak for himself; and his own writings are a magnificent vindication of his person and work.

Yet just as the reading of Scripture does not automatically cause all criticisms of it to evaporate, so Luther's writings do not in themselves eliminate superficial or perverse analyses of him. The poetical ideal expressed by Horace, *De mortuis nihil nisi bonum,* has seldom been followed, particularly in the treatment of men like Luther whose controversial ideas and acts have elicited violent opposition. In point of fact, the dead — even those who were most adroit in defending their interests while alive — are pitifully at the mercy of their critics after their demise. What our Lord said to Peter concerning old age applies with equal force to death: "When thou wast young, thou girdedst thyself, and walkedst wither thou wouldest: but when thou shalt be old, thou shalt stretch forth thy hands, and another shall gird thee, and carry thee wither thou wouldest not." Little study of the history of Luther interpretation is needed to demonstrate beyond all question that the Reformer, powerful enough in life to intimidate popes and emperors, has been "girded" again and again with viewpoints appallingly inimical to his true beliefs and has continually been "carried whither he wouldest not" since his death.[1]

The extent to which even today such interpretative tyrannizing grossly corrupts a Luther no longer able to defend his own interests is sufficiently illustrated by a single example: John Osborne's dramatic hit "Luther," in which Albert Finney presented a coherent (and hopelessly unhistorical) portrait of the Reformer as one driven by unconscious psychological motivations outside of his volitional control. Osborne derived his picture of Luther from the influential psychoanalytical study of the Reformer by the distinguished Harvard lecturer Erik Erikson: *Young Man Luther,* whose translations into European languages have made it equally known on the continent. On the ground of Luther's supposed hatred for a father whom he wished unconsciously to repudiate, Erikson claims that the young Reformer successfully worked through his personal "identity crisis" by transferring the attributes of his father to the Pope and all spiritual authority; once he had dealt with his own unsolved problem of self-hate and intolerance of disobedience by destroying these prime authority symbols, Luther "was at last able to forgive God for being a Father, and grant Him justification."[2] Thus through an indecisive modicum of historical data concerning Luther's relations with childhood authority figures, together with a liberal and uncritical dose of aprioristic Freudian scientism, students and playgoers in our day have been introduced to a Luther who has only the vaguest connection with the actual Wittenberg Reformer. Can we imagine what Luther himself while alive would have done to an interpretation of his cardinal doctrine of justification (the justification of the *sinner* by God's grace through faith) which asserted that God was the *recipient* of Luther's forgiveness and justification? But victories over the dead are easy conquests; and it is the purpose of this volume to render them

---

[1] See, inter alia: Richard Stauffer, *Le Catholicisme à la découverte de Luther* (Neuchâtel: Delachaux et Niestlé, 1966); Otto H. Pesch, "Twenty Years of Catholic Luther Research," *Lutheran World,* XIII/3 (1966); Marc Lienhard, "Les recherches actuelles sur Luther," *Revue d'Histoire et de Philosophie Religieuses,* XLVII/3 (1967); Jaroslav Pelikan (ed.), *Interpreters of Luther: Essays in Honor of Wilhelm Pauck* (Philadelphia: Fortress Press, 1968).

[2] Erik H. Erikson, *Young Man Luther: A Study in Psychoanalysis and History* (New York: W. W. Norton, 1958), p. 222.

considerably less facile where the greatest of the Reformers is concerned.

An effort is made in the chapters which follow to defend Luther from a variety of classic and contemporary criticisms arising not only in the theological, but also in the scientific, literary, and political domains. In the first part of the book, we show that Luther's view of Holy Writ can in no sense be identified with the current existentializing of Biblical authority and that his general theological thrust is directly relevant to the present "secular" crisis in religious discussion. The second section of the volume argues that Luther, far from being a scientific reactionary and opponent of the Copernican system, in fact encouraged scientific investigation through his theological insights. Next, the Reformer is vindicated from the criticism expressed by Erasmus and reiterated to the present day that "wherever Luther's teaching prevails, there one sees the downfall of learning." In the fourth part of the book, I deal with Shirer's amazing contention in his *Rise and Fall of the Third Reich* that Luther was the spiritual father of Hitler's blood and soil policy and genocidic treatment of the Jews; and I contrast Luther's true orientation with the present-day totalitarian conditions in East Germany as I have myself observed them. Finally returning to the "Queen of the sciences," I show that in diametric contrast to an alleged tension between Luther's theology and missionary endeavor, the former provides the strongest incentive to the realization of the latter.

Hopefully the present work will serve, in the afterglow of the 450th anniversary of the Reformation, to reinforce lines written by 19th century English poet Robert Montgomery:

> Chief o'er all the galaxy of lights
> Which stud the firmament of Christian fame,
> Shone Luther forth —that miracle of men!
> A Gospel Hero, who with faith sublime
> Fulmined the lightnings of God's flaming Word
> Full on the towers of superstitions' home,
> Till lo! they crumbled; and his withering flash
> Yet sears the ruin with victorious play.[3]

JOHN WARWICK MONTGOMERY

6 January 1970
The Epiphany of Our Lord

---

[3] Quoted in P. C. Croll (ed.), *Tributes to the Memory of Martin Luther* (Philadelphia: G. W. Frederick, 1884), pp. 62-63. Cf. Albert Greiner, *Martin Luther ou l'hymne à la grâce* (Paris: Plon, 1966).

I

LUTHER'S THEOLOGY TODAY

A. THE 95 THESES THEN AND NOW

B. LUTHER'S HERMENEUTIC
VS.
THE NEW HERMENEUTIC

A.

THE 95 THESES THEN AND NOW

"Out of love and zeal for the elucidation of truth, the following theses will be debated . . . in the name of our Lord Jesus Christ," wrote an obscure monk at the head of a series of propositions four and a half centuries ago. Those theses were posted not simply on a Castle Church door (which the ravages of time have long since claimed) but on the conscience of Christendom. Both the formal theology and the practical church activity of Luther's day were leading men away from, rather than to, Christ's salvation, for the Church had embraced the greatest error of all: the belief that man can earn his own way to Life. "Love and zeal for the elucidation of truth" demand that this same fundamental error — today appearing in a different but no less deadly form — be revealed for what it is. So that readers may compare these theses, number by number, with the originals, some of which have been freely used in various degrees of modification, Luther's Theses are printed in the column headed "Then" and those of the present writer in that headed "Now."

THEN

1. Our Lord and Master Jesus Christ, in saying, "Repent ye," etc., intended that the whole life of believers should be penitence.

2. This word cannot be understood of sacramental penance, that is, of the confession and satisfaction which are performed under the ministry of priests.

3. It does not, however, refer solely to inward penitence; nay, such inward penitence is naught unless it outwardly produces various mortifications of the flesh.

4. The penalty thus continues as long as the hatred of self — that is, true inward penitence — continues, namely, till our entrance into the kingdom of heaven.

5. The Pope has neither the will nor the power to remit any penalties except those which he has imposed by his own authority or by that of the canons.

6. The Pope has no power to remit any guilt except by declaring or warranting it to have been remitted by God or, at most, by remitting cases reserved for himself; in which cases, if his power were despised, guilt would certainly remain.

7. God never remits any man's guilt without at the same time subjecting him, humbled in all things, to the authority of His representative, the priest.

8. The penitential canons are imposed only on the living, and according to them no burden ought to be imposed on the dying.

9. Hence the Holy Spirit acting in the Pope does well for us, in that, in his decrees, he always makes exception of the article of death and of necessity.

10. Those priests act wrongly and unlearnedly who, in the case of the dying, reserve the canonical penances for purgatory.

11. Those tares about changing the canonical penalties into the penalty of purgatory surely seem to have been sown while the bishops were asleep.

NOW

1. Our Lord and Master Jesus Christ, in saying: "Repent ye," etc., intended that the whole life of believers should be penitence.

2. In the sixteenth century, indulgences diverted men from a life of repentance; in the mid-twentieth century, "secular religion" achieves the same purpose.

3. Then the world was kept from the Gospel by hyper-religiosity on the part of churchmen; now, by their hyper-irreligiosity.

4. Which is another way of saying that false religion and irreligion amount to the same thing.

5. The lamentable condition Bonhoeffer called "cheap grace" can result either from selling grace cheaply (as then) or from cheapening the very idea of grace (as now).

6. Grace is cheapened and man becomes his own pseudo-savior when God is considered dead — either metaphorically or literally — for as God diminishes, man assumes His place.

7. Yet true religion begins with the Baptist's affirmation: "He must increase, but I must decrease."

8. A world without a name for God is a world without a name for salvation; all hope in such a world is man-made hope and therefore chimerical.

9. Secular towers of Babel, built over the alleged coffin of Deity, invariably produce confusion of tongues.

10. A "secular Christ" is a contradiction in terms, for He plainly said: "My kingdom is not of this world."

11. The way is narrow and the gate strait leading to that Kingdom; to enter it, one must give up all hope of saving oneself and rely fully upon the Christ.

THEN

12. Formerly the canonical penalties were imposed not after, but before absolution, as tests of true contrition.

13. The dying pay all penalties by death and are already dead to the canon laws and are by right relieved from them.

14. The imperfect soundness or charity of a dying person necessarily brings with it great fear, and the less it is, the greater the fear it brings.

15. This fear and horror are sufficient by themselves, to say nothing of other things, to constitute the pains of purgatory, since it is very near to the horror of despair.

16. Hell, purgatory, and heaven appear to differ as despair, near-despair, and peace of mind differ.

17. With souls in purgatory, seemingly, it must needs be so, that, as horror diminishes, charity increases.

18. Nor does it seem to be proved, by any reasoning or any Scriptures, that they are outside of the state of merit or of the increase of charity.

19. Nor does this appear to be proved, that they are sure and confident of their own blessedness, at least not all of them, though we may be very sure of it.

20. Therefore the Pope, when he speaks of the plenary remission of all penalties, does not mean simply of all, but only of those imposed by himself.

21. Thus those preachers of indulgences are in error who say that by the indulgences of the Pope a man is loosed and saved from all punishment.

22. For in fact he remits to souls in purgatory no penalty which, according to the canons, they would have had to pay in this life.

23. If any entire remission of all penalties can be granted to anyone, it is certain that it is granted to none but the most perfect, that is, to very few.

NOW

12. To rely on Christ is to take Him at His Word.

13. To question His teachings at any point is to stand in judgment upon one's Judge and Advocate.

14. To translate the Christ of the New Testament into a secular "man for others" is to re-do God in our image instead of permitting Him to re-do us in His image.

15. If the Christ in whom one believes is unable to say, "He who has seen Me has seen the Father," He is no Christ at all.

16. A "fully kenotic Christ" is by definition unknowable.

17. If nonetheless believed in, a "fully hidden Christ" will necessarily turn out to be the mirror-image of His worshiper or of the times in which the worshiper lives.

18. Salvation through such a Christ is self-salvation, which is in reality damnation.

19. If we are on the threshold of a "new age of the Spirit," we had better be sure which "spirit" he is before we worship him; the spirit of the age is generally "the god of this world."

20. "Test the spirits," says Scripture, intending that God's Word judge the spirit of the age.

21. But when Scripture itself is judged, what ultimate judgment remains?

22. Human judgment of Scripture assumes that we know more than God and must in the last analysis save ourselves.

23. Indeed, all "secular theology" is grounded in an optimistic view of man's abilities.

THEN

24. Hence the greater part of the people must needs be deceived by this indiscriminate and high-sounding promise of release from penalties.

25. The same powers which the Pope has over purgatory in general, every bishop has in his own diocese, and, in particular, every curate in his own parish.

26. The Pope acts most rightly in granting remission to souls, not by the power of the keys (which is of no avail in this case), but by way of suffrage.

27. They preach human doctrine who say that the soul flies out of purgatory as soon as the money thrown into the chest rattles.

28. It is certain that when the money rattles in the chest, avarice and gain may be increased, but the suffrage of the Church depends on the will of God alone.

29. Who knows whether all the souls in purgatory desire to be redeemed from it, according to the story told of Saints Severinus and Paschal?

30. No man is sure of the reality of his own contrition, much less of the attainment of plenary remission.

31. Rare as is a true penitent, so rare is one who truly buys indulgences, that is to say, most rare.

32. Those who believe that through letters of pardon they are made sure of their own salvation will be eternally damned along with their teachers.

33. We must especially beware of those who say that these pardons from the Pope are that inestimable gift of God by which man is reconciled to God.

NOW

24. How quickly has theology in our century come the full circle from modernistic optimism to secularistic optimism!

25. How very fast sinners forget the piles of eyeglasses and teeth and the bodies of naked children at Dachau.

26. How readily sinners forget that apart from the living God of Scripture and His Son's death in our behalf, we turn our secular existence into a seething cauldron of hell and hatred.

27. They preach human doctrine who say that the soul achieves bliss as soon as the divine truths of Biblical Christianity are reduced to "secular cash-value."

28. What is achieved is "sinful cash-value," nothing less, nothing more.

29. One wallows in secularity, without hope of a solution for its self-centered condition.

30. In the words of Tillich, one destroys proper theological correlation by turning revelational answers into existential questions.

31. Unless a clear and unimpeachable Word from outside the human situation is available to man, his existential predicament will remain overwhelming and secular optimism will stand revealed as naïve folly.

32. Those who believe that they are made sure of their own salvation by "finding God where the social action is" will be eternally damned along with their teachers.

33. We must especially beware of those who say that such social and political action is that inestimable gift of God by which men are reconciled.

THEN

34. For the grace conveyed by these pardons has respect only to the penalties of sacramental satisfaction, which are of human appointment.

35. They preach no Christian doctrine who teach that contrition is not necessary for those who buy souls out of purgatory or buy confessional licenses.

36. Every Christian who feels true compunction over his sins has plenary remission of pain and guilt, even without letters of indulgence.

37. Every true Christian, whether living or dead, has a share in all the benefits of Christ and of the Church, given him by God, even without letters of indulgence.

38. The remission, however, imparted by the Pope is by no means to be despised, since it is, as I have said, a declaration of divine remission.

39. It is a most difficult thing, even for the most learned theologians, to exalt before the people the great riches of indulgences and, at the same time, the necessity of true contrition.

40. True contrition seeks and loves punishment, while the ampleness of pardon relaxes it and causes men to hate it or at least gives them occasion for them to do so.

41. Apostolic pardons ought to be purchased with caution, lest the people falsely suppose that they are to be preferred to other good works of charity.

42. Christians should be taught that it is not the mind of the Pope that the buying of indulgences is to be in any way compared with works of mercy.

43 Christians should be taught that he who gives to a poor man or lends to a needy man does better than if he buys indulgences.

NOW

34. The "horizontal" reconciliation of man with man depends squarely upon the "vertical" reconciliation of God and man at the Cross, even as the Second Table of the Decalogue follows and rests on the First.

35. They preach no Christian doctrine who teach that contrition and faith in Christ are not necessary for doing God's will in society.

36. Every Christian who feels true compunction over his sins has plenary remission of pain and guilt, even without involvement in social and political causes.

37. Involvement in politics and society will follow as a fruit of faith, for "we love because He first loved us."

38. But when the Christ-relationship is not seen as the ground of Christian social action, Law is confused with Gospel, and neither faith nor properly motivated social action remains.

39. It is a most difficult thing, even for the most learned theologians, to exalt before the people the great riches of political action and, at the same time, the necessity of true contrition.

40. True contrition accepts chastisement for its sins, while stress on changing society makes it seem relatively unimportant.

41. It is well to remember that the Great Commission had to do with the proclamation of the Gospel, not the reformation of the Roman Empire.

42. The Empire was much transformed through the Gospel, but where this occurred it happened because believers "sought first the Kingdom of God and his righteousness."

43. Christians should be taught that he who proclaims to a man an eternal word of grace does better than he who participates in a sit-in.

THEN

44. For by a work of charity, charity increases, and man becomes better, while by means of indulgences he does not become better, but only freer from punishment.

45. Christians should be taught that he who sees anyone in need and, passing him by, gives money for indulgences is not purchasing the indulgence of the Pope, but calls down upon himself the wrath of God.

46. Christians should be taught that unless they have superfluous wealth, they are bound to keep what is necessary for the use of their own households and by no means to lavish it on indulgences.

47. Christians should be taught that while they are free to buy indulgences, they are not commanded to do so.

48. Christians should be taught that the Pope, in granting indulgences, has both more need and more desire that devout prayer should be made for him than that money should be freely paid.

49. Christians should be taught that the Pope's indulgences are useful if they do not put their trust in them, but most hurtful if through them they lose the fear of God.

50. Christians should be taught that if the Pope knew of the exactions of the preachers of indulgences, he would rather see the Basilica of St. Peter burned to ashes than that it should be built up with the skin, flesh, and bones of his sheep.

51. Christians should be taught that the Pope, as is his duty, would rather, if necessary, sell the Basilica of St. Peter and give of his own money to those from whom the preachers of indulgences extract money.

52. Vain is the hope of salvation through letters of indulgence, even if a commissary — nay, the Pope himself — were to pledge his own soul for them.

NOW

44. For by a preachment of God's Word, which never returns void, the believer grows in sanctification, while by sit-ins man does not become better but only less subject to adverse social conditions.

45. Christians should be taught that he who substitutes political lobbying for the proclamation of divine grace is not obtaining God's favor but calls down upon himself God's wrath.

46. Christians should be taught that he who does not perform charitable acts to his immediate neighbor accomplishes little in attempting to improve the lot of those at a distance.

47. Christians should be taught that while they are free to engage in social and political action, they are not commanded to do so for their soul's salvation.

48. Scripture nowhere sets forth a normative political or social system; Christians are to proclaim the eternal riches of Christ under political systems of the "right" and of the "left."

49. Christians should be taught that political and social philosophies are useful if they do not put their trust in them, but most hurtful if through them they lose the fear of God.

50. Adherence neither to the "American way of life" — conservative or liberal — nor to socialism nor to Communism will save or damn a man; adherence to Christ, and Christ alone, saves, and rejection of Him, and Him alone, damns.

51. To demand that all Christians accept a given political or social philosophy as a test of "consistent Christianity" is to elevate man's word to the level of God's Word.

52. Vain is the hope of salvation through secular activity, even if a divinity-school dean — nay, the President of the World Council of Churches himself — were to pledge his own soul for it.

THEN

53. They are enemies of Christ and of the Pope who, in order that indulgences may be preached, condemn the Word of God to utter silence in their churches.

54. Wrong is done to the Word of God when in a sermon as much time is spent on indulgences as on God's Word, or even more.

55. The mind of the Pope cannot but be that if indulgences, which are a very small matter, are celebrated with single bells, single processions, and single ceremonies, the Gospel, which is a very great matter, should be preached with a hundred bells, a hundred processions, and a hundred ceremonies.

56. The treasures of the Church, whence the Pope grants indulgences, are neither sufficiently named or known among the people of Christ.

57. It is clear that they are at least not temporal treasures; for these are not so readily lavished, but only accumulated by many of the preachers.

58. Nor are they the merits of Christ and of the saints; for these, independently of the Pope, are always working grace to the inner man and the cross, death, and hell to the outer man.

59. St. Lawrence said that the treasures of the Church are the poor of the Church; but he spoke according to the use of the word in his time.

60. We are not speaking rashly when we say that the keys of the Church, bestowed through the merits of Christ, are that treasure.

61. For it is clear that the power of the Pope alone is sufficient for the remission of penalties and of reserved cases.

NOW

53. They are enemies of Christ and of the Church who, in order that a secular salvation may be preached, condemn the Word of God to utter silence in their churches.

54. Wrong is done to the Word of God when in a sermon as much time is spent on secular topics as on God's Word, or even more.

55. If secular participation by Christians is celebrated with single bells, single processions, and single ceremonies, the Gospel should be preached with a hundred bells, a hundred processions, and a hundred ceremonies.

56. A theology derived from the sinful human situation will be humanistic and sinful, likewise an ethic stemming from man's situation instead of from God's revelation.

57. A "contextual" or "situation" ethic foolishly assumes that proper norms will automatically arise from descriptive action; this is a precise example of what G. E. Moore called the "naturalistic fallacy."

58. If human "contexts" and "situations" are self-centered, will not the ethic found there have the same qualities? Can water rise above its source?

59. The importing of *agape*-love into a situation as a norm is of little help apart from God's revealed law, for *agape* is a motive, not a guide for specific action; it will be interpreted in whatever direction the sinful interpreter wishes.

60. How ironical that churchmen today combine "absolute" social and political programs with relativistic situational ethics! Is this not the predictable imbalance of Paul's "natural man"?

61. Only the eternal Word of God can show the relative to be truly relative (e.g., political systems) and the absolute to be truly absolute (e.g., God's moral law).

THEN

62. The true treasure of the Church is the holy Gospel of the glory and grace of God.

63. This treasure, however, is deservedly most hateful because it causes the first to be the last.

64. But the treasure of indulgences is deservedly the most acceptable because it causes the last to be the first.

65. Hence the treasures of the Gospel are nets wherewith of old they have fished for men of means.

66. The treasures of indulgences are nets wherewith they now fish for the means of men.

67. Those indulgences which the preachers loudly proclaim to be the greatest graces are seen to be truly such as regard the promotion of gain.

68. Yet they are in reality in no degree to be compared with the grace of God and the piety of the Cross.

69. Bishops and curates ought to receive the commissaries of apostolic pardons with all reverence.

70. But they are still more bound to open their eyes and ears lest these men preach their own dreams in place of the Pope's commission.

71. He who speaks against the truth of apostolic pardons, let him be anathema and accursed.

72. But he, on the other hand, who is seriously concerned about the wantonness and licenses of speech of the preachers of pardons, let him be blessed.

73. As the Pope justly thunders against those who use any kind of contrivance to the injury of the traffic in pardons.

74. Thus, indeed, much more, it is his intention to thunder against those who, under the pretext of granting indulgences, use contrivances to the injury of holy charity and of truth.

NOW

62. The true treasure of the Church is still the holy Gospel of the glory and grace of God.

63. This treasure, however, is understandably — today as yesterday — most hateful because it causes the first to be the last.

64. But salvation through secularity is understandably the most acceptable because it causes the last to be the first.

65. Hence the treasures of the Gospel are nets wherewith churchmen of old have fished to save men from a sinful society.

66. The treasures of secularity are nets wherewith churchmen now fish for acceptance by a sinful society.

67. Those activities which the preachers loudly proclaim to be the greatest graces are seen to be truly such as appeal most to unregenerate standards.

68. They are in reality in no degree to be compared with the grace of God and the piety of the Cross.

69. Christians ought to receive with all reverence exhortations to racial justice, open housing, and equality before the law, for these are demonstrably the will of the God of scriptural revelation.

70. But they are still more bound to open their eyes and ears lest churchmen preach their own fancies in place of the Biblical Word.

71. He who speaks against legitimate and proper social action, let him be anathema and accursed.

72. But he, on the other hand, who is seriously concerned about the wantonness and licenses of speech of the preachers of social action, let him be blessed.

73. We should justly thunder against those who by rationalization impede the advance of social justice.

74. And, much more, we should thunder against those who, under the cloak of social programs, depreciate the proclamation of divine grace and the Gospel message.

THEN

75. To think that papal indulgences have such power that they could absolve a man even if — to mention an impossibility — he had violated the Mother of God, is madness.

76. We affirm, on the contrary, that papal indulgences cannot take away even the least of venial sins as regards its guilt.

77. The saying that, even if St. Peter were now Pope, he could grant no greater graces, is blasphemy against St. Peter and the Pope.

78. We affirm, on the contrary, that both he and any other Pope has greater graces to grant, namely, the Gospel, powers, gifts of healing, etc. 1 Cor. 12:6, 9.

79. To say that the cross set up among the insignia of the papal arms is of equal power with the Cross of Christ is blasphemy.

80. Those bishops, curates, and theologians who allow such discourses to have currency among the people will have to render an account for this.

81. This license in the preaching of pardons makes it no easy thing, even for learned men, to protect the reverence due to the Pope against the calumnies or, at all events, the keen questioning of the laity.

82. For instance: Why does not the Pope empty purgatory for the sake of most holy charity and of the supreme necessity of souls — this being the most just of all reasons — if he redeems an infinite number of souls for the sake of that most perishable thing, money, to be spent on building a basilica — this being a very slight reason?

83 Again: Why do funeral masses and anniversary masses for the deceased continue, and why does not the Pope return, or permit the withdrawal of, funds bequeathed for this purpose, since it is wrong to pray for those who are already redeemed?

NOW

75. To think that secular involvement has such power that it can absolve a man even if he denies the atoning death and bodily resurrection of God's Son, is madness.

76. We affirm, on the contrary, that all of man's good works cannot take away even the least of venial sins as regards its guilt.

77. The saying that Jesus was "the most" — the ideal man and "the place to be" — but not, as He claimed, the very incarnate God, is blasphemy.

78. We affirm that the true grace the Lord Christ has to grant is not a program but Himself: His death for our sins and His resurrection for our justification.

79. To say that any earthly goal is of equal rank with the Cross of Christ is blasphemy.

80. Those bishops, curates, and theologians who allow such ideas to have currency among the people will have to render an account for this.

81. The preaching of "secular Christianity" today makes it no easy thing, even for learned men, to protect the reverence due the visible church against the calumnies of unbelievers and the criticisms of the laity.

82. For instance: Why do the secular theologians always claim credit for jumping on social bandwagons that have been put into motion outside the Church?

83. Again: Why bother with all the theological jargon if Christianity really reduces to humanism?

THEN

84. Again: What new kind of holiness of God and the Pope is it to permit an impious man and an enemy of God, for money's sake, to redeem a pious soul, which is loved by God, and not rather to redeem this pious soul, which is loved by God, out of free charity, for the sake of its own need?

85. Again: Why is it that the penitential canons, long since abrogated and dead in themselves, in very fact and because of non-use, are still redeemed with money, through the granting of indulgences, as if they were still valid.

86. Again: Why does not the Pope, whose riches are at this day more ample than those of the wealthiest of the wealthy, build the one Basilica of St. Peter with his own money rather than with that of poor believers?

87. Again: Why does the Pope grant indulgences to those who, through perfect contrition, have a right to plenary remissions and indulgences?

88. Again: How much greater would be the benefit accruing to the Church if the Pope, instead of once, as he does now, would bestow these remissions and indulgences a hundred times a day on any one of the faithful?

89. Since it is the salvation of souls, rather than money, that the Pope seeks by granting indulgences, why does he suspend the letters and indulgences granted long ago, since they are equally efficacious?

90. Repressing these scruples and arguments of the laity by force alone and not solving them by giving reasons for so doing is to expose the Church and the Pope to the ridicule of their enemies and to make Christian men unhappy.

91. If, then, indulgences were preached according to the spirit and mind of the Pope, all these questions would be resolved with ease; nay, they would not exist.

NOW

84. Again: Why not study sociology or politics or psychiatry instead of attempting to be a sloppy representative of these fields with irrelevant theological training?

85. Again: If the Church's beliefs are derived from the fallible human situation like everyone else's, why does the Church presume to judge others or declare grace to them?

86. Again: If God is *ipso facto* "where the action is," was He motivating the action of the Third Reich, as National Socialist theologians said He was?

87. Again: If the theologian judges the Bible and its Christ, who judges the theologian?

88. Again: When Christ demanded fidelity to the "once for all" character of His saving work, how is it that the contemporary Church is satisfied only when it continually proclaims "some new thing"?

89. And how does it happen that faithful preaching of the eternal Word of grace is despised, while the most bizarre theological and ecclesiastical innovations are lauded to the skies as a true mark of "relevance"?

90. Repressing these scruples and arguments is to expose the Church to the ridicule of her enemies and to make Christian men unhappy.

91. If, then, churchmen would subordinate themselves to God's Word, and seek first to bring their wills into accord with Christ's will, and make His Gospel their Gospel, all other things would be added, and the troubles of today's Church would be resolved with ease; nay, they would not exist.

THEN

92. Away, then, with all those prophets who say to the people of Christ, "Peace, peace!" though there is no peace.

93. Blessed be all those prophets who say to the people of Christ, "The cross, the cross," and there is no cross.

94. Christians should be exhorted to strive to follow Christ, their Head, through pain, death, and hell;

95. And thus to enter heaven through many tribulations rather than in the security of peace.

NOW

92. Away, then, with all those prophets who say to the people of Christ, "Peace, peace!" though there is no peace.

93. Blessed be all those prophets who say to the people of Christ, "The cross, the cross," and there is no cross.

94. Christians should be exhorted to strive to follow Christ, their Head, through pain, death, and hell;

95. And thus to enter heaven through the tribulations of His cross rather than in the pseudo-security of optimistic secularity.

B.
LUTHER'S HERMENEUTIC
VS.
THE NEW HERMENEUTIC

"For many years, the hermeneutic problem, alongside that of the 'historical Jesus,' has been the focal issue of Protestant theology." So wrote Jesuit theologian René Marlé as he observed the Protestant scene in 1963.[1] The next years marked an even greater intensification of interest in the hermeneutic question, as is well evidenced by the appearance of an American counterpart to Gerhard Ebeling's *Zeitschrift für Theologie und Kirche*, the first volume of which is titled *The Bultmann School of Biblical Interpretation: New Directions?*[2] The Autumn 1965 issue of *Dialog* is appropriately devoted to "Biblical Interpretation," and there we find Samuel Laeuchli of the Garrett Theological Seminary noting the crucial nature of the present hermeneutic quest: "After even a superficial study of the questions involved, one comes rather soon to one's senses, realizing that in this pertinent debate a great deal is at stake — the meaning of Scriptural language, the possibility of a theological discipline, and above all, the task of preaching and teaching in the church and to the world."[3]

Laeuchli is not exaggerating: the very possibility of the theological enterprise and the continuance of evangelical proclamation depend squarely upon the church's response to current hermeneutic issues. Because hermeneutics is no longer seen as an isolated and rather prosaic subbranch of exegetical theology but as the focal point of all the theological disciplines — as

[1] René Marlé, *Le Problème théologique de l'herméneutique: Les grands axes de la recherche contemporaine* (Paris: Editions de l'Orante, 1963) p.7: "Le problème de l'herméneutique est, depuis plusieurs années, à côté de celui du 'Jésus historique,' le problème le plus souvént traité au sein de la théologie protestante."

[2] James M. Robinson et al., *The Bultmann School of Biblical Interpretation: New Directions?* Vol. I of *Journal for Theology and the Church* (New York: Harper Torchbooks, 1965).

[3] Samuel Laeuchli, "Issues in the Quest of a Hermeneutic," *Dialog*, IV (Autumn 1965), 250.

the key to the overall relation of Word and faith,[4] the church that takes a misstep here may well find itself fatally committed to heresy or to irrelevance. Thus it behooves us in all seriousness to examine the approaches to the hermeneutic task being advocated today and to compare them with Scripture and with the hermeneutical heritage of the Reformation.

The present essay endeavors to provide such a comparison, with special reference to the Lutheran hermeneutic. It is this essayist's conviction that far too little of present hermeneutic discussion takes into account the church's past wrestlings with interpretive problems. How readily we forget Bernard of Chartres' sage words: "We are like dwarfs sitting on the shoulders of giants. When, therefore, we see more and farther than the ancients, it is neither because of the sharpness of our vision nor as a result of our individual height; it is solely because they carry us on their shoulders and give us the benefit of their tremendous stature."[5] The insights of the Reformation, above all, must not be neglected in our contemporary hermeneutic quest, for that epoch wrestled most tenaciously and heroically with the core problems of Biblical interpretation and application.

Our first task will be to obtain a clear picture of the mid-20th-century hermeneutic stance in Protestantism. Next we shall observe the manner in which the contemporary hermeneutic movement understands Luther's approach to Scripture; and this in turn will lead to a reexamination of the Lutheran hermeneutic. Finally we shall take a hard doctrinal and epistemological look at the current hermeneutic orientation and pose the unavoidable question of confessional limits as regards the employment of interpretive methodology.

THE LEITMOTIV OF CONTEMPORARY HERMENEUTICS

Is it possible to arrive at any single characterization of

---

[4] See especially Gerhard Ebeling's programmatic essay, "The Significance of the Critical Historical Method for Church and Theology in Protestantism," which appeared in *Zeitschrift für Theologie und Kirche*, XLVII (1950), 11 ff., when the journal was reestablished under Ebeling's editorship; the same essay may be consulted in Ebeling's *Wort und Glaube* (Tübingen: J. C. B. Mohr, 1960), pp. 12 ff., and in its English translation, *Word and Faith* (Philadelphia: Fortress Press, 1963), pp. 27 ff.

[5] Quoted in Etienne Gilson, *L'Esprit de la philosophie médiévale*, 2d ed. (Paris: Librairie Philosophique J. Vrin, 1944), p. 402: "Nous sommes comme des nains assis sur les épaules de géants. Nous voyons donc plus de choses que les Anciens, et de plus lointaines, mais ce n'est ni par l'acuité de notre vue, ni par la hauteur de notre taille, c'est seulement qu'ils nous portent et nous haussent de leur hauteur gigantesque."

Protestant hermeneutics today? The bewildering variety of theological approaches both in Europe and in America would seem to militate against any unified hermeneutic theme. Bultmann's successor at Marburg, Werner Georg Kümmel, sees no less than five distinct orientations in European New Testament scholarship, not counting "orthodox" Barthians and Bultmannians:[6] (1) conservatives (e.g., Karl Heinrich Rengstorf of Münster), (2) *Heilsgeschichte* scholars (e.g., Kümmel himself), (3) the post-Bultmannian group (including Ernst Fuchs, Gerhard Ebeling, Hans Conzelmann, Ernst Käsemann, and Günther Bornkamm, as well as the more individualistic Heinrich Ott), (4) the Pannenberg school, led by the young Mainz theologian Wolfhart Pannenberg, and (5) independents, whose views defy group categorization (e.g., Ethelbert Stauffer, Helmut Thielicke, and Oscar Cullmann). And if these several groupings were not sufficiently intimidating, we can remind ourselves that they leave out contemporary American theological thought entirely! Yet I do believe that a single hermeneutic orientation can be traced in current theology. To find it we must set forth the hermeneutic thrust of individual European and American theologians and then observe the common thread binding them together. Our survey, though necessarily cursory, will endeavor to render faithfully the hermeneutic perspective of the views discussed; references to primary and secondary literature will offer avenues for further study to those wishing it.

Rudolf Bultmann

We begin with Rudolf Bultmann, whose preoccupation with hermeneutics has probably been the single most important factor in bringing about the overwhelming current interest in the subject. Bultmann sets forth his hermeneutical position most clearly in his essay, "Is Exegesis Without Presuppositions Possible?"[7] His answer: Though exegesis must not presuppose its results, it can never dispense with the method of historical-critical research (including the nonmiraculous view of the universe that sees "the whole historical process as a closed unity") or with an existential "life relation" between Scriptural text and the interpreter him-

---

[6] Kümmel presented this typology in discussion with Carl F. H. Henry; see the latter's "European Theology Today," *Faith and Thought: Journal of the Victoria Institute*, XCIV (Spring 1965), 9—91, especially p. 12.

[7] Rudolf Bultmann, "Ist voraussetzungslose Exegese möglich?" *Theologische Zeitschrift*, XIII (1957), 409—17; English translation in *Existence and Faith: Shorter Writings of Rudolf Bultmann*, ed. Schubert M. Ogden (New York: Meridian Living Age Books, 1960), pp.289—96.

self; thus all Biblical interpretation involves a necessary circularity (the so-called "hermeneutical circle" embracing text and exegete), and no exegesis can properly be regarded as "objective."[8]

> The validity of Bultmann's hermeneutics depends on whether or not he is right when he says that to speak of God is simultaneously to speak of oneself. That is, hermeneutics — when its object is to understand the meaning of Christian faith in the Bible — deals with history, and one cannot interpret history validly from some distant, disengaged vantage point. . . . We can now see in what terms Bultmann is willing to speak of the Bible as authoritative: the Bible is authoritative only in so far as it communicates the claim (*Anspruch*) of God on me and thus leads me to radical obedience in faith. It is authoritative in so far as it calls into question my previous self-understanding and leads me to a new self-understanding — from seeing myself as one who must and perhaps can make his own way to seeing myself as a sinner before God who by God's now occurring act of grace has been given new life with an openness to the future.[9]

Karl Barth

Barth roundly condemns Bultmann's claim that before interpreting Scripture one has to "put on the armor" of Heidegger's existential philosophy. Implicitly in his *Church Dogmatics* and explicitly in his *Rudolph Bultmann: Ein Versuch ihn zu verstehen*,[10] Barth sets himself against such a hermeneutic — which for him is nothing less than a return to the Old Liberalism.

---

[8] Cf. on Bultmann's circularity principle Armin Henry Limper, "Hermeneutics and Eschatology: Rudolf Bultmann's Interpretation of John, Chapters 13—17" (unpublished Ph.D. dissertation, The Divinity School, University of Chicago, 1960), and John Warwick Montgomery, "The Fourth Gospel Yesterday and Today," *Concordia Theological Monthly*, XXXIV (April 1963), 203—205.

[9] Jackson Forstman, "Bultmann's Conception and Use of Scripture," *Interpretation*, XVII (1963), 459—61. The same point is made in greater detail and with even more force in chap. i ("Qu'est-ce que l' 'objectivité'?") of André Malet, *Mythos et logos: La pensée de Rudolf Bultmann*, Lettre-préface de R. Bultmann (Genève: Labor et Fides, 1962), pp. 5—19.

[10] Karl Barth, *Rudolf Bultmann: Ein Versuch ihn zu verstehen* (Zollikon-Zürich: Evangelischer Verlag, 1952).

Barth rejects the Bultmannian notion of a normative *Vorver-ständnis* brought to Scripture from the outside; the interpreter, says Barth, must allow the Bible to act as a "catalyst" on his powers of comprehension, thereby modifying and refining the preconceptions he brings to the reading of Scripture.[11]

Yet, as the Italian scholar Riverso has cogently shown, Barth never succeeded in completely ridding his own theology of existential-dialectic elements.[12] Thus he is as willing as Bultmann to admit that neutral investigation of *Historie* will never yield a resurrected Christ (for Barth the "objectivity" of the *heilsgeschichtliche* Resurrection is discovered only in the faith relation).[13] Barth's position, we are told, "disposes of many difficulties arising from the intellectualist bedevilment of the concept of faith, and sets it clearly in the context of existential encounter and response. . . . Although the New Testament message is often formulated 'Jesus is the Christ,' the Object of faith is not doctrinal propositions about Jesus, but the divine presence or objectivity encountered in Him."[14] Since truth is conceived as personal encounter with the Christ of Scripture and not as the propositional affirmations of the Bible, the Biblical writers "can be at fault in every word, and have been at fault in every word, and yet according to the same scriptural witness, being justified and sanctified by grace alone, they have still spoken the Word of God in their fallible and erring human word."[15] Not unlike Bultmann, Barth asserts: "The Bible is God's Word so far as

---

[11] See the excellent comparative treatment of Bultmann and Barth on the problem of hermeneutical *Vorverständnis* by Jesuit L. Malevez, "Exegèse biblique et philosophie," *Nouvelle Revue Théologique*, LXXVIII (Nov.-Dec. 1956), 897—914, 1027—42; English translation as Appendix II to Malevez, *The Christian Message and Myth: The Theology of Rudolf Bultmann* (Westminster, Md.: Newman Press, 1958), pp. 168—212.

[12] Emmanuele Riverso, *La teologia esistenzialistica di Karl Barth: Analisi, interpretazione e discussione del sistema* (Napoli, 1955). Bouillard agrees, though for various reasons he is not happy with the flat characterization of Barth as an "existentialist": "Certes, cette théologie [de Barth] offre des aspects existentialistes (au sens très large de ce mot): son auteur lui-même en convient [D. III, 4. viii; *Bultmann*, p. 38]" — Henri Bouillard, *Karl Barth*, III (Paris: Aubier, 1957), 298—99.

[13] See John Warwick Montgomery, "Karl Barth and Contemporary Theology of History," *The Cresset*, XXVII (Nov. 1963), 8—14, now published in the author's *Where Is History Going?* (Grand Rapids, Mich.: Zondervan, 1969), chap. v.

[14] James Brown, *Kierkegaard, Heidegger, Buber and Barth: Subject and Object in Modern Theology* (New York: Collier Books, 1962), pp. 145—46.

[15] Karl Barth, *Church Dogmatics* (Edinburgh: T. & T. Clark, 1936—), I, Part 2, 529 to 30.

God lets it be His Word, so far as God speaks through it."[16]
Well recognizing the ecumenical implications of this view for
dialog with Roman Catholicism, Robert McAfee Brown declares
that Barth "delivers us from what can be a very perverse notion
of *sola Scriptura* that would assert that we go to the Bible and
to the Bible alone, as though in the process we could really by-
pass tradition. He delivers us from a kind of Biblicism that is
content to rest simply with a parroting of the vindication, 'the
Bible says.'"[17] And the eminent Jesuit theologian Gustave
Weigel perceptively notes that for Barth

> Scripture is the word of God, not in the sense
> that its propositions are spoken by God, but in
> the sense that the vision of the men who wrote
> the words points efficaciously to the transcendent
> Lord God. Barth does not give an exegesis of
> the Scriptures, but gives the existentialist mean-
> ing of the Biblical narratives.[18]

In Barth's approach to Biblical interpretation, then, the
"hermeneutical circle" of text and interpreter remains unbroken
in spite of his opposition to Bultmann, and it is only through
the existential dynamic of the hermeneutic situation that a fallible

----

[16] Ibid., I, Pt. 1, 123. For an excellent discussion of this and related passages in Barth's *Church Dogmatics* see Robert D. Preus, "The Word of God
in the Theology of Karl Barth," *Concordia Theological Monthly,* XXXI (Feb.
1960), 105—15.

[17] Robert McAfee Brown, "Scripture and Tradition in the Theology of
Karl Barth," in Leonard J. Swidler, ed., *Scripture and Ecumenism: Protestant, Catholic, Orthodox and Jewish* (Pittsburgh; Duquesne University Press,
1965), p. 42.

[18] Gustave Weigel, *A Survey of Protestant Theology in Our Day* (Westminster, Md.: Newman Press, 1954), p. 33. Weigel's remarks on p. 30 are
also to the point here: "Barth especially is interested in a return to the reformers, not to the content of their teaching, but merely to their starting
point. Against the liberals, Barth and Brunner go back to the Bible as the
Word of God, and they free the theological enterprise from the chains of
philological method in order to achieve the true meaning of the Scriptures,
which philology cannot detect. Against the Orthodox, the Neo-Orthodox
reject any Biblicism whereby verbal inspiration or literal inerrancy condemn the theologian to make affirmations that have nothing to do with God.
Seemingly, therefore, the Neo-Orthodox are a Center theology, but a closer
examination of their thought has led many critics to believe that they are
basically liberals in a strange guise. In America Neo-Orthodoxy in the
Barthian manner is not popular, though his work is sufficiently known. The
paradoxical character of such thought is bewildering because the constant
linking of 'Yes' and 'No,' with no possibility of bringing them into some
kind of unified synthesis, leaves the student dizzy."

book becomes God's Word and revelatory. Only when we see this fully can we appreciate Oscar Cullmann's recent about-face: his refusal any longer to support the Barthian hermeneutic that would give philological and historical exegesis merely a preliminary role to theological interpretation proper. Cullmann observes that Barth is especially exposed to the danger of uncontrolled theological speculation "à cause de la richesse de sa pensée," and in order to avoid this danger of allowing the existential situation or theological tradition to engulf the clear teaching of Scripture, Cullmann now opts for objective philological treatment of the text throughout all exegetical operations.[19]

Post-Bultmannians

The most influential movement in European theology today is variously called "post-Bultmannianism" and "the New Hermeneutic." Bultmann's satisfaction with the mere "thatness" of the historical Jesus — his unwillingness to pursue the historical question beyond the perspective of the early church's interpretation of Jesus — has impelled a number of his students to engage in a hermeneutic quest for a more meaningful conjunction of the Jesus of history with the Christ of the early church. Wide differences exist among the post-Bultmannians (e.g., between Fuchs and Ott), but they are united in their endeavor to connect faith and history hermeneutically. Though they have departed from their master in many respects, they all maintain the centrality of Bultmann's "hermeneutical circle" and his conviction that an objective identification of the Biblical text with God's Word is a manifestation of unfaith. Thus Ernst Käsemann writes:

> In New Testament language we are driven to test
> the spirits even within Scripture itself. We can-
> not simply accept a dogma or a system of doc-
> trine but are placed in a situation vis-à-vis
> Scripture which is, at the same time and in-
> separably, both responsibility and freedom.
> Only to such an attitude can the Word of God
> reveal itself in Scripture; and that Word, as

---

[19] Oscar Cullmann, "La nécessité et la fonction de l'exégèse philologique et historique de la Bible," in Jean Boisset, et al., Le Problème biblique dans le Protestantisme (Paris: Presses Universitaires de France, 1955), pp. 131-47. Cullmann here disavows the Barthian position on "theological exegesis" that he advocated in "Les problèmes posés par la méthode exégétique de l'école de Karl Barth," Revue d'Histoire et de Philosophie Religieuses, VIII (Jan.—Feb. 1928), 70—83.

> Biblical criticism makes plain, has no existence
> in the realm of the objective — that is, outside
> our act of decision.[20]

Gerhard Ebeling is doubtless the most influential spirit of the New Hermeneutic. For him systematic theology has as its subject matter "the word event itself, in which the reality of man comes true," and by "word event" is meant "the event of interpretation";[21] theology, then, has its source in the hermeneutic circle embracing Biblical text and existentially grounded interpreter.[22] In reviewing Ebeling's *Das Wesen des christlichen Glaubens*,[23] James M. Robinson uses the term "neo-liberalism" to describe his position and notes that "although Ebeling devotes chapters to most of the traditional doctrines, he would not refer to these as the objects of faith. Faith is not to be bifurcated into the believer and his beliefs on the analogy of the scientist and his objects of study, that is, the subject-object pattern of scientific epistemology is not applicable for faith."[24] Marlé offers in much the same terms a fuller analysis of Ebeling's conscious break with the hermeneutic of orthodox Protestantism:

> For him, the fundamental error of Protestant
> orthodoxy (and doubtless, in his view, the error
> of all orthodoxy) has been to consider the Word
> of God independently of its actualization in
> preaching — to make it in some way an object
> instead of seeing a movement there. That is
> why, moreover, orthodoxy could not recognize
> the peculiarly theological importance of herme-
> neutics. For hermeneutics is precisely that which
> permits the Word of God to be truly Word, in

[20] Ernst Käsemann, *Exegetische Versuche und Besinnungen*, I (2d ed.; Göttingen: Vandenhoeck und Ruprecht, 1960), 232—33; English translation in Käsemann's *Essays on New Testament Themes*, in Studies in Biblical Theology, No. 41 (London: SCM Press, 1964), p. 58.

[21] Gerhard Ebeling, *Theologie und Verkündigung; Ein Gespräch mit Rudolf Bultmann*, in Hermeneutische Untersuchungen zur Theologie, I (Tübingen: J. C. B. Mohr, 1962), 14 to 15. Cf. James M. Robinson and John B. Cobb, Jr., eds., *The New Hermeneutic*, in New Frontiers in Theology, II (New York: Harper & Row, 1964), *passim*.

[22] Ebeling discusses the hermeneutical circle in his *Wort und Glaube*, p. 337.

[23] Gerhard Ebeling, *Das Wesen des christlichen Glaubens* (Tübingen: J. C. B. Mohr, 1959); trans. R. G. Smith, *The Nature of Faith*, (London: Collins, 1961).

[24] James M. Robinson, "Neo-Liberalism," *Interpretation*, XV (Oct. 1961), 488.

other words to attain its meaning, by conjoining with the one to whom it is addressed. . . . The [Protestant] perspective was transformed from the day when hermeneutics was no longer regarded as the simple application of rules external to the reality concerned, but as the way of disclosing that reality from the inside. According to Ebeling, the role of Heidegger and of Bultmann has been determinative in this regard. For both — and Ebeling resolutely follows in their wake — hermeneutics expresses a relationship to reality, allowing that reality to express itself, indeed, to realize its meaning.[25]

In Ernst Fuchs the "dynamic" (vs. orthodox propositional) concept of the Word seems to attain its zenith. By a hermeneutical principle Fuchs means the situation in which one places something to see what it really is, thereby allowing it to display its meaning; so, for example, to find out what a cat is, put it in front of a mouse.[26] Scripture, then, cannot be interpreted objectively; it must be placed into dynamic, existential relation with its theological interpreter. Instead of being objectified, the Word actively objectifies everything else while forever remaining subject. "Freedom for the Word" is manifested not in reliance on objective history or on a propositionally inerrant text but in a staking of everything on the Word of love.[27] Fuch's hypostatizing of language is but a logical outcome of the post-Bultmannian rejection of the subject-object distinction, but it gives to his writings such an air of mystical unreality that he is much less frequently quoted than his confrère Ebeling. Marlé devotes but three sentences to him (in the last footnote of his book); for those surprised at his neglect of Fuchs — especially for those students of Fuchs who would see in him the most profound theologian of the New Hermeneutic — Marlé must confess that he

---

[25] Marlé, pp. 88—89.

[26] Ernst Fuchs, *Hermeneutik* (Bad Cannstatt: R. Müllerschön, 1954), pp. 103—18.

[27] See Fuchs, "Was wird in der Exegese interpretiert?" in his *Zur Frage nach dem historischen Jesus*, in Gesammelte Aufsätze, No. 2 (Tübingen: J. C. B. Mohr, 1960), pp. 286 ff.; trans. Andrew Scobie, *Studies of the Historical Jesus*, in Studies in Biblical Theology, No. 42 (London: SCM Press, 1964), pp. 84 ff. A semi-popular work directly reflecting Fuch's hermeneutic approach is Heinz Zahrnt, *Es begann mit Jesus von Nazareth* (Stuttgart: Kreuz-Verlag, 1960); trans. J. S. Bowden, *The Historical Jesus* (New York: Harper & Row, 1963).

has found in Fuchs "much obscurity, a multitude of viewpoints more rapidly touched on than given depth treatment, and a most abstract terminology, the original force of which has escaped us."[28]

Heinrich Ott, Karl Barth's successor at Basel, rejects "the so-called 'subject-object schema' and the view that all thinking and language to a very great extent necessarily have an objectifying character";[29] he goes so far as to assert that "the objective mode of knowledge is entirely inappropriate to historical reality because there are no such things as objectively verifiable facts, and, secondly, that all true knowledge of history is finally knowledge by encounter and confrontation."[30] Ott's attempt to re-pristinate Heidegger theologically will be evident from these existential (and virtually solipsistic) assertions that intentionally eliminate the possibility of an objective Biblical hermeneutic.[31]

The practical exegetical consequences of the post-Bultmannian hermeneutic can be seen in the work of Hans Conzelmann and Günther Bornkamm. Conzelmann regards the New Testament writers as free reshapers of the Jesus tradition; thus Luke's own existential stance produces a "subordinationist" portrait of Jesus, and Luke "deliberately takes the 'today' [Lk. 4:21] which is expressed in this passage [Mk. 2:19] as belong-

---

[28] Marlé, p. 139.

[29] Heinrich Ott, "Was ist systematische Theologie?" *Zeitschrift für Theologie und Kirche*, LVIII, Beiheft 2 (Sept. 1961), p. 32; English translation in James M. Robinson and John B. Cobb, Jr., eds., *The Later Heidegger and Theology*, in New Frontiers in Theology I (New York: Harper & Row, 1963), 93.

[30] Heinrich Ott, *Die Frage nach dem historischen Jesus und die Ontologie der Geschichte* (Zürich: EVZ-Verlag, 1960); English translation in Carl E. Braaten and Roy A. Harrisville, eds., *The Historical Jesus and the Kerygmatic Christ* (New York: Abingdon, 1964), p. 148. Readers of the present essay may be interested to learn that an orthodox Reformation counterweight to the Braaten-Harrisville symposium has been published under the title, *Jesus of Nazareth: Savior and Lord* (Grand Rapids, Mich.: Eerdmans, 1966). Carl F. H. Henry is the editor, and this essayist provides the concluding chapter, "Toward a Christian Philosophy of History."

[31] For a valuable insight into Ott's most recent thinking, see Robert W. Funk's report of the Second Drew University Consultation on Hermeneutics (April 9—11, 1964), in which Ott participated; the report was published under the title "Colloquium on Hermeneutics," *Theology Today*, XXI (Oct. 1964), 287—306. Funk succinctly summarizes Ott's position as follows: "Ott continues to attempt to mediate between Barth and Bultmann, as he did in his early works. He has increasingly taken his cues from the later Heidegger in endeavoring to work out a theological program which transcends the subject-object dichotomy and is thus nonobjectifying in character." (p. 289)

ing to the past, and builds up the picture of Jesus' whole career on the basis of this historical interpretation."[32] Discrepancies and historical-geographical blunders are rife in Luke's Gospel, for Conzelmann does not hold to any kind of propositional inspiration. A single example will suffice:

> The locality of the Baptist becomes remarkably vague. Luke can associate him neither with Judea nor with Galilee, for these are both areas of Jesus' activity. Yet on the other hand there has to be some connection, so the Baptist is placed on the border. It is obvious that Luke has no exact knowledge of the area, and this is why he can make such a straightforward symbolical use of localities.
>
> He creates a further discrepancy by introducing a motif of his own: in place of the Pharisees and Sadducees he puts the ὄχλοι [Luke 3:7].[33]

Günther Bornkamm's *Jesus of Nazareth*[34] leaves one in little doubt as to the effect of the New Hermeneutic on Biblical theology. In a penetrating review of this book, Otto Piper of Princeton writes:

> The English translation has been hailed by some American scholars as "the best presentation of Jesus that we have" and as an "event in the intellectual history of our time." May this reviewer be forgiven for dissenting from the views of his esteemed colleagues. . . .
>
> This new position . . . does not differ in principle from Bultmann's: Though faith is not necessarily to be understood in existentialist terms, nonetheless the theologian has already arrived at the knowledge of the religious truth before he opened his New Testament, and consequently everything in the Gospels that is not

---

[32] Hans Conzelmann, *The Theology of Saint Luke,* trans. Geoffrey Buswell (London: Faber and Faber, 1960), pp. 170—71.

[33] Ibid., p. 20.

[34] Bornkamm, *Jesus of Nazareth,* trans. Irene and Fraser McLuskey (New York: Harper & Row, 1960).

fit to illustrate this truth is *a priori* doomed to
be rejected.[35]

Paul J. Achtemeier, in evaluating the post-Bultmannian
"New Quest," finds the whole movement riddled with unex-
amined and perilous *a prioris;* it is in fact a revival of the ancient
heresy of Docetism.

> We have, in short, the anomalous fact that the
> new quest of the historical Jesus is being carried
> on by a group of men who would have to regard
> any valid historical fact about Jesus of Nazareth
> as threatening the purity of the Christian faith.
> That the renewed search is carried on within a
> perspective that contains such a strange contra-
> diction would seem to indicate that the move-
> ment, as now conceived, can hardly reach con-
> clusive results.[36]

This antipathy to objective data among the post-Bultmannians is quite understandable in the light of our preceding
discussion: these theologians are simply working out the logical
implications of the hermeneutical circle — the "dynamic interaction" of text and interpreter — that appears in varying degrees in virtually all of contemporary theology.

American Lutheranism

Leaving the European scene,[37] we hasten on to America,
particularly to the Lutheran theological situation in our own
country. Is the same nonpropositional, nonobjective view of
Biblical interpretation in evidence here? The answer is very
definitely, "Yes." Examples could be multiplied; we shall restrict
ourselves only to the more prominent. As early as 1948 Joseph

---

[35] Otto A. Piper, "A Unitary God with Jesus as His First Theologian,"
Interpretation, XV (Oct. 1961), 473-74. For further evidences of Born-
kamm's aprioristic exegesis, see Bornkamm, G. Barth, and H. J. Held,
Tradition and Interpretation in Matthew, trans. Percy Scott (London: SCM
Press, 1963).

[36] Paul J. Achtemeier, "Is the New Quest Docetic?" *Theology Today,* XIX
(Oct. 1962), 364.

[37] It will be noted that we have not discussed the hermeneutics of those
European theologians whom Kümmel considers conservative or independent
(see above, the text at note 6). If more space were at our disposal, we could
show that even the most orthodox of these theologians balk at an unqualified, objective identification of the historical Scripture with God's Word. For
Kümmel and the *Heilsgeschichte* school, as for the positions we have dis-

Sittler endeavored to reorient Lutherans from a verbal, "static" approach to the Bible, to a "dynamic," "instrumental" understanding of God' Word.

> All verbal forms, all means of communication through speech, prove too weak for this massive bestowal [of Revelation]. . . . We must ask after the Word of God in the same way faith asks after Jesus Christ. That is to say, that the Word of God *becomes* Word of God for us. . . . To assert the inerrancy of the text of scripture is to elevate to a normative position an arbitrary theological construction.[38]

Martin Heinecken has consistently approached the problem of Biblical interpretation from the standpoint of Kierkegaard's existentialism. In *The Moment Before God,* Heinecken's most influential book, truth is identified with paradoxical subjectivity, faith is understood as blind "encounter with the unknown," and the objective historical accuracy of the Biblical text is considered totally irrelevant to Christian commitment.

> It is thus impossible to find an objectively certain basis for the revelation of God in Christ. Again, Kierkegaard's prophetic insight is apparent in the controversies waged over the in-

cussed above, divine revelation "exists only in response" (quoted in Carl F. H. Henry, *Faith and Thought: Journal of the Victoria Institute,* XCIV, 34) and must not be viewed propositionally. Rengstorf and the "conservatives" seem to use the Holy Spirit as a kind of *deus ex machina* to bolster an epistemologically weak hermeneutic (see Karl Heinrich Rengstorf, *Die Auferstehung Jesu,* 4th ed. [Witten/Ruhr: Luther-Verlag, 1960], p. 109). Stauffer properly recognizes the necessity of an objective treatment of the Gospel record (see Ethelbert Stauffer, *Jesus and His Story,* trans. Richard and Clara Winston [New York: Knopf, 1960]) but handles most of the theological concepts of the Bible as mythical motifs (cf. Krister Stendahl's comments in the text at note 52 below). Pannenberg and Thielicke, though their theologies are a healthly corrective to the current existential-dialectic mainstream, draw the line at inerrant Biblical authority. And Cullmann, whose theology is perhaps the most attractive of all, while categorically refusing to view the resurrection of Christ (or any link in the temporal sequence of salvation history) as mythical, nonetheless regards the Fall and the ultimate Eschaton as Biblical myths (see, on Cullmann, Jean Frisque, *Oscar Cullmann: Une théologie de l'histoire du salut* [Tournai, (Belgique:) Castermann, 1960], and the critical remarks in Gustaf Wingren, *Creation and Law,* trans. Ross Mackenzie [Edinburgh: Oliver and Boyd, 1961], *passim*).

[38] Joseph Sittler, *The Doctrine of the Word* (Philadelphia: Muhlenberg Press, 1948), pp. 62—63, 68 (Sittler's italics).

> spiration, inerrancy, and infallibility of the Bible. Fundamentalists, who staked everything on a repudiation of higher criticism, have definitely lost the battle. As far as any merely historical facts can be established with a degree of certainty, the composite character of many of the books of the Bible is established. Yet the witness of faith is not thereby affected. . . . A very radical critic of the Bible may really be a "believer" if he makes the proper distinctions and does not try to bolster with irrelevant argument that which must be "believed" in a transformation of existence.[39]

That the "dynamic" (as opposed to "propositional") view of Scripture is now quite well established in Lutheran theological circles in the United States is evident from the 1963 symposium volume, *Theology in the Life of the Church,* to which 14 members of the Conference of Lutheran Professors of Theology contributed essays. In the chapter dealing with "The Bible," Warren Quanbeck of Luther Seminary considers hopelessly outmoded the conviction of Protestant orthodoxy that Scripture is "a collection of revealed propositions unfolding the truth about God, the world, and man" and that "because the Holy Spirit was the real author of Scripture, every proposition in it was guaranteed infallible and inerrant, not only in spiritual, but in secular matters."[40] For Quanbeck, Biblical exegesis requires the hermeneutic assumption that "since human language is always relative, being conditioned by its historical development and usage, there can be no absolute expression of the truth even in the language of theology. Truth is made known in Jesus Christ, who is God's Word, his address to mankind. Christ is the only absolute."[41]

The very recent introduction of the post-Bultmannian New Hermeneutic into the American theological scene is doing much

---

[39] Martin J. Heinecken, *The Moment Before God* (Philadelphia: Muhlenberg Press, 1956), p. 262. In his Foreword the author writes: "It has been asserted that this book is not so much about Kierkegaard as it is an expression of my own views. This is cheerfully admitted" (p. vii). "Cheerfully" is hardly *le mot juste,* however, since the vital objectifying elements in Kierkegaard are totally neglected in Heinecken's interpretation of him.

[40] *Theology in the Life of the Church,* ed. Robert W. Bertram (Philadelphia: Fortress Press, 1963), p. 23.

[41] Ibid., p. 25.

to reinforce and deepen the theological stance represented by such older Lutheran theologians as Sittler, Heinecken, and Quanbeck. The focal center of the "young Turks" is *Dialog,* the Lutheran theological journal begun in 1962 under the editorship of Carl E. Braaten of the Lutheran School of Theology in Chicago. Two other members of the editorial staff whose frequent contributions set the tone of the journal are Roy A. Harrisville of Luther Seminary and Robert W. Jenson of Luther College. Significantly, Braaten wrote his doctoral dissertation on Martin Kähler (1835—1912), who "with apparently equal justification can be viewed as a forerunner of either Karl Barth or Rudolf Bultmann"[42] and whose "influence cuts across such varied theologies as those of Tillich, Barth, Brunner, and Bultmann."[43] In a Foreword to Braaten's partial translation of Kähler's *Der sogenannte historische Jesus und der geschichtliche, biblische Christus,* Paul Tillich makes the revealing assertion: "I do believe that one emphasis in Kähler's answer is decisive for our present situation, namely, the necessity to make the certainty of faith independent of the unavoidable incertitudes of historical research."[44] Braaten agrees, and stresses the fact that Kähler rejected the objective approach to Biblical interpretation characteristic of Protestant orthodoxy:

> Kähler felt that the orthodox definition of faith involving the sequence of *notitia, assensus,* and *fiducia* led to an intellectualistic regimentation of the *ordo salutis.* Volitional assent to intellectual information about God and Christ was made a prerequisite of saving faith. This information was to be found in the Bible and was secured by the doctrine of verbal inspiration. This attempt of Protestant Orthodoxy to provide a threshold of objectivity over which a person must pass to enter the household of faith was particularly offensive to Kähler. . . . [For him] the Bible is nothing less than the Word of God to those who believe in Christ. . . . With Kähler's christological view of biblical authority it was possible to arbitrate the painfully fruitless

---

[42] Martin Kähler, *The So-called Historical Jesus and the Historic, Biblical Christ,* trans. and ed. Carl E. Braaten (Philadelphia: Fortress Press, 1964), p. 2.

[43] Ibid., p. 33.

[44] Ibid., p. xii.

> discussion about whether everything in the
> Bible or only parts of it are the Word of God.
> The first alternative can be set aside by a re-
> *ductio ad absurdum.*[45]

Harrisville, who has flatly stated in a *Dialog* article, "we admit to the discrepancies and the broken connections in Scripture,"[46] is the co-editor with Braaten of two volumes that endeavor through translations of current German theological articles to introduce American theologians to post-Bultmannian trends. In the second of these anthologies,[47] Harrisville himself writes a paper in which he, like his European counterparts, rejects the subject-object distinction in hermeneutics and history and classes attempts to operate with an objective text as throwbacks to the liberal "life of Jesus" era.[48] Jenson, a critic of the present essayist for his belief in plenary inspiration,[49] likewise blurs the hermeneutic task by interlacing Biblical text with "dogmatic tradition" and with "the live questions of our present existence"; thus, for him, "even the profoundest reading and understanding of the Bible will not in itself give us a message to proclaim," and "at the moment when we must speak, Scripture provides no guarantee that we will speak rightly."[50]

And now, what of the question with which this section began? How can the numerous positions here described be related to one another? We might point out the clear historical connections; for example, Heinz Kimmerle has shown that Wilhelm Dilthey, on whom Martin Heidegger and Bultmann based

---

[45] Ibid., pp. 17—18, 31.

[46] Roy A. Harrisville, "A Theology of Rediscovery," *Dialog,* II (Summer 1963), 190. Harrisville's book, *His Hidden Grace: An Essay on Biblical Criticism* (New York: Abingdon, 1965), is an attempt to make the higher criticism of Scripture palatable if not attractive to clergymen schooled in classical Lutheran theology.

[47] Cited in note 30 above. The first is Carl E. Braaten and Roy A. Harrisville, *Kerygma and History: A Symposium on the Theology of Rudolf Bultmann* (New York: Abingdon Press, 1962).

[48] Harrisville, "Representative American Lives of Jesus," *The Historical Jesus and the Kerygmatic Christ,* pp. 172—96.

[49] Robert W. Jenson, "Barth Weak on Scripture?" *Dialog,* I (Autumn 1962), 57—58; this is a comment on my report, "Barth in Chicago: Kerygmatic Strength and Epistemological Weakness," *Dialog,* I (Autumn 1962), 56—57.

[50] Jenson, "An Hermeneutical Apology for Systematics," *Dialog,* IV (Autumn 1965), 269, 274. Jenson has specialized in Barth; see his *Alpha and Omega: A study in the Theology of Karl Barth* (New York: Thomas Nelson, 1963).

their existentialisms, derived his hermeneutic from the later Friedrich Schleiermacher[51] — thus a chain is forged from the subjective psychologism of Schleiermacher (from which Ritschlian modernism grew) to the post-Bultmannian New Hermeneutic. And we have already noted the dependence of Barth as well as Bultmann on Martin Kähler, whose distinction between *Geschichte* and *Historie* places Biblical theology in a nonobjective frame of reference. But such historical connections, though they evidence a relationship among the positions we have discussed, do not tell us precisely what that relationship is.

On Dec. 30, 1957, at the annual meeting of the Society of Biblical Literature, a symposium was held on "Problems in Biblical Hermeneutics." Two papers at that symposium, both presented by advocates of the new approach in Biblical study, set forth in bold strokes the core connections among the views we have been treating. Let us hear first from Lutheran Krister Stendahl of Harvard:

> Recent studies by Käsemann, Dahl, Bornkamm, Stauffer, and others have reopened the question about the historical Jesus and tried to indicate the necessity of overcoming our defeatism at this point. This has great significance for historical studies but for the problem of interpretation in terms of hermeneutics it seems to remain a fact that by and large we have to approach Jesus in the traditions about him, not the traditions about him in the light of factual historical information. . . .
>
> This state of affairs has a tendency to cut two ways: It has led to the strange situation where modern biblical studies deal with the traditional theological concepts of incarnation, miracles, redemption, justification, election, and all the rest in a language which causes some old liberals to shiver and leads the listeners to many

---

[51] Cf. James M. Robinson, "Hermeneutic Since Barth," in his *The New Hermeneutic*, pp. 70—71. Kimmerle is a student of the Dilthey critic Hans-Georg Gadamer, who, though he is trying to give an "ontological turn" to hermeneutics by concentrating on linguistic understanding rather than existential psychology, nevertheless (like Dilthey) takes the hermeneutical circle for granted, asserting that "historic tradition can only be understood by recalling the basic continuing concretizing taking place in the continuation of things." (*Wahrheit und Methode: Grundzüge einer philosophischen Hermeneutik* [Tübingen: J. C. B. Mohr, 1960], p. 355)

modern preachers to believe that the liberal era of doubt and disbelief is finally overcome once and for all. Yet the preacher as well as the scholar knows — or should know — that he is expounding *traditions*, the faith of the Church in Christ, while people might think that he is telling them the simple facts about Jesus of Nazareth. In the long run it must become clear that the situation which has allowed this kind of double talk and has made it possible to capitalize on the distance between "sender" and "receiver," is actually based on an insight into the nature of the biblical material which is more radical in its positivism than that of the liberals.[52]

Thus modern Biblical hermeneutics has shifted its concern from Scripture as a record of objective fact to Scripture as a compendium of traditions reflecting the faith stance of the writers. It has in consequence become possible to use traditional Biblical-theological terminology without committing oneself to the veracity of the events or interpretations involved; and this admitted "double talk" is actually more radical than the old liberalism.[53]

Another speaker at the SBL symposium, J. Coert Rylaarsdam of the University of Chicago Divinity School, has rendered contemporary theology, liberal and conservative, an immense service by spelling out explicitly the radical and unbridgeable chasm separating the hermeneutics of Reformation orthodoxy from the hermeneutics of 20th-century Protestantism. The following paragraphs cannot receive too close attention:

For orthodoxy the forms and processes of revelation were summed up in the contents of the Bible and in the form of events it reported. The Bible was called "the objective Word of God," or "the Word of God written." It was revelation, rather than faith's testimony to reve-

---

[52] Krister Stendahl, "Implications of Form-Criticism and Tradition-Criticism for Biblical Interpretation," *Journal of Biblical Literature,* LXXVII (March 1958), 34—36.

[53] A good example of this nonfactual, "dramatic-mythical" treatment of traditional Biblical concepts is provided by the Norwegian Lutheran New Testament scholar Ragnar Leivestad in his *Christ the Conqueror; Ideas of Conflict and Victory in the New Testament* (London: SPCK, 1954).

lation. The paradox between revelation and biblical history was wiped out in like manner. Orthodoxy not only said God revealed himself in history, but also that there was a bit of history which was revelation. To be sure, this bit of history was set apart, not subject to the laws of history in general, and so, in a sense, irrelevant for it. But, chronologically and materially, revelation was history. The Nile turned into real blood; and every first-born son in Egypt really died. This may or may not be so; but for orthodoxy the meaning of revelation depended on it. There was no gap between fact and faith. Fact demanded faith and the dependence of faith on fact is not paradoxical, but absolute. The integrity and factual accuracy of the Bible is the guarantee for the history on which faith rests.

The most distinctive feature of the current theological emphasis is its dynamic view of revelation. This is not only true of its neo-orthodox wing; it is equally true of the successors of liberalism; or, for that matter, in such Jewish theologians as Buber and Heschel. Revelation is not a static form with a stable content, subject to descriptive analysis; it is a dynamic action, existentially apprehended, the source of faith and inspired response. Revelation, *per se,* is not subject to analysis. Deeply aware of the conditionedness of all forms, material and intellectual, contemporary theology shies away from equating any of them with revelation. Relativism, long with us, plays a more radical role than ever before. Forms may be the media of revelation; they are an inevitable outcome of it. They can serve as a clue to its meaning; but, as such, forms are never revelation. To use the technical term, there is a paradoxical relationship between the action of God, which is revelation, and all objective structures and processes that are patient of descriptive analysis.[54]

---

[54] J. Coert Rylaarsdam, "The Problem of Faith and History in Biblical Interpretation," *Journal of Biblical Literature,* LXXVII (March 1958), 27—29.

Here we have not only a clear and precise statement of the classical Protestant hermeneutic stance but also a lucid description of the ideological thread uniting contemporary hermeneutical positions from Barth to the post-Bultmannians. For orthodoxy the Bible in its entirety is God's objective revelation, and both the events and the interpretations comprising it are veracious; faith accepts and is grounded in the propositional validity of the Scriptural text, and all sound exegesis of the Bible must proceed from this presuppositional base. For contemporary hermeneutics, however, the text of Scripture cannot be understood as objective, historically veracious revelation separated from the exegete (the subject-object distinction); an existential-dialectical relation between text and interpreter (the hermeneutical circle) has to be assumed; and since God's revelation can never be equated with the Scriptural text, hermeneutical affirmations will necessarily have a paradoxical quality, and relativism will "play a more radical role than ever before." In brief, for orthodox Protestantism the Bible has stood as an unblemished historical revelation, objectively distinguishable from its interpreters, who in order to understand it must allow it to interpret itself apart from the existential orientations reflected in church tradition or in the mind-set of the exegete; but for 20th-century hermeneutics the Bible, as a fallible witness to revelation, cannot be qualitatively distinguished from its interpreters, past or present, and to understand it we must recognize the relativistic dialectic that connects us as interpreters with the text we endeavor to interpret.

Luther's Hermeneutic in Fiction and in Fact

Having obtained a detailed picture of the contemporary Protestant hermeneutic scene, we can now benefit from a historical analysis of Reformation Lutheranism's interpretive approach to Holy Writ. Our particular concern is to discover whether the confessional roots of Lutheranism encourage, permit, or reject the existential-dialectic hermeneutics of present-day Protestant (not excluding Lutheran) thought. Since a theological wedge is frequently driven today between Luther and the representatives of classical Lutheran orthodoxy,[55] emphasis will be placed here on Luther himself. This is not to say that we agree with the stereotyped criticisms of the much maligned orthodox

---

[55] See Jaroslav Pelikan, *From Luther to Kierkegaard* (St. Louis, Mo.: Concordia Publishing House, 1950), *passim,* and the present essayist's editorial Introduction to *Chytraeus on Sacrifice* (St. Louis, Mo.: Concordia Publishing House, 1962).

theologians; indeed, criticism of them is but the first step toward criticism of Luther and of the Confessions, for as C. S. Lewis

LAST EDITION OF LUTHER'S BIBLE TRANSLATION WHICH
HE HIMSELF SAW THROUGH THE PRESS

well noted in reference to the 19th-century Tübingen-school attack on Paul as a perverter of Jesus' teachings:

> In the earlier history of every rebellion there is
> a stage at which you do not yet attack the
> King in person. You say, "The King is all
> right. It is his Ministers who are wrong. They
> misrepresent him and corrupt all his plans —

> which, I'm sure, are good plans if only the
> Ministers would let them take effect." And
> the first victory consists in beheading a few
> Ministers: only at a later stage do you go on
> and behead the King himself.[56]

But considerations of space prohibit our dealing here with
the hermeneutics of classical orthodoxy. Presumably, in any case,
it will be granted that if Luther manifests a thoroughgoing "orthodox" hermeneutic, his orthodoxist followers are deserving of
no more condemnation than he is.

At present, however, the advocates of the modern hermeneutical stance have no interest in criticizing Luther; quite the
opposite, for they claim that he is a forerunner of the very interpretive approach they are supporting. So, for many years, it
has been fashionable to associate Luther with Kierkegaard, the
theological father of existentialism.[57] Along the same line, Sittler unfavorably compares the hermeneutic of Protestant orthodoxy with "Luther's dialectical understanding of the Word":

> The post-Reformation theologians did not under-
> stand the Scriptures in this way. They failed
> sufficiently to ponder the fact that the Bible,
> when it speaks of revelation, points beyond itself
> to an event to which it bears witness, but which
> is not the Bible itself. Luther's theological
> concern was directed toward this event, this
> divine self-disclosure, to which the Bible is a
> a singular and incomparable witness. But
> Luther did not equate Scripture with the divine
> event.[58]

Luther's Christological approach to the Bible is supposed to
have freed him from static, plenary inspiration and given him
an existentially dynamic hermeneutic; thus Quanbeck interprets
Luther's view:

---

[56] C. S. Lewis' Introduction to J. B. Phillips, *Letters to Young Churches*
(New York: Macmillan, 1948), p. x.

[57] See, for example, Heinecken, *The Moment Before God, passim.*

[58] Sittler, pp. 34—35. Sittler relies here on Philip S. Watson, *Let God Be
God* (London: Epworth Press, 1947), a secondary source of generally high
quality, which, however, leaves something to be desired in its treatment of
Luther's doctrine of the Word. A more recent work presenting essentially
the same interpretation of Luther's Biblical hermeneutic is Willem Jan
Kooiman, *Luther and the Bible,* trans. John Schmidt (Philadelphia: Muhlenberg Press, 1961).

The apprehension of the Bible in static or mechanical terms is necessarily inadequate. The reader must approach it as a dynamic and personal message in which he is himself existentially involved in order to experience its purpose and power. . . .

Luther's view of the authority of Scripture differs greatly from that of the Middle Ages. For the Occamist theologian, Scripture is authoritative because every word in it has been inspired by the Holy Spirit. This is true of the Lutheran scholastics also, with the significant difference that, standing on Luther's shoulders, they rejected the fourfold interpretation and insisted on the historical sense of Scripture. Luther stands apart from both groups. Scripture is his authority because it reveals Jesus Christ, because in it God speaks His Word of judgment and grace.[59]

(Note here that the proportion is created: Medieval exegesis is to Luther's exegesis as the propositional, plenary inspiration of Lutheran orthodoxy is to an existential hermeneutic. We shall see very shortly how the terms of this proportion must be exactly reversed!) This same general evaluation of Luther is shared by a recent student of his Galatians commentary who claims that, in contrast to Calvin, Luther's "interpretations tend to be subjective, directed toward the individual, existential life of the believer"; accordingly Luther's hermeneutic principles can "lead to an extreme — to a subjectivism (as in Schleiermacher or Bultmann) which stresses the religious feeling or the existential (personal) dimensions of subjective faith over against the object of faith, thus losing what Prenter calls Luther's 'realism'."[60]

For most of contemporary Biblical scholarship, however, as Rylaarsdam has made clear, stress on "the existential (personal) dimensions of subjective faith over against the object of faith"

---

[59] Warren A. Quanbeck, "Luther's Early Exegesis," in Roland H. Bainton, et al., *Luther Today* in Martin Luther Lectures, I (Decorah, Iowa: Luther College Press, 1957), pp. 92, 99.

[60] Thomas D. Parker, "The Interpretation of Scripture. I. A Comparison of Calvin and Luther on Galatians," *Interpretation*, XVII (Jan. 1963), 68, 75. Interestingly enough, Sittler, in his *Doctrine of the Word*, takes a diametrically opposite tack by claiming that Calvin as well as Luther maintained Sittler's dialectic-existential view of the Word (pp. 27—32).

is anything but an "extreme." Thus no time has been lost in endeavoring to bring Luther into the very midst of the Bultmannian and post-Bultmannian hermeneutic camp. Bultmann's interpreters have consistently claimed that in him "one sees in unmistakable outlines the shadow of Luther,"[61] for just as Luther saw the inadequacy of man's moral efforts toward salvation, so (we are told) Bultmann sees the inadequacy of man's "intellectual" efforts to "justify himself" by way of a propositionally inerrant Scripture.[62]

The post-Bultmannian advocates of the New Hermeneutic have been especially vocal in claiming Luther as their spiritual father. The following comment by Käsemann is typical:

> Neither miracle nor the canon nor the Jesus of history is able to give security to our faith. For our faith there can be no objectivity in this sense. That is the finding which New Testament scholarship has made plain in its own fashion. But this finding is only the obverse of that acknowledgment which Luther's exposition of the third article of the Creed expresses.[63]

Ebeling has made Luther one of his specialties; his *Habilitationsschrift* in fact dealt with the Reformer's hermeneutics.[64] We are therefore justified in including a rather long quotation from Ebeling — a quotation which shows with crystal clarity how Luther has been drawn into the orbit of the nonpropositional, existential, circular, "word-event" hermeneutic:

> The fundamental problem for him is not a verbal description of God but the exposure of man's existence before God; that is to say, the proclamation of God's judgment over man. With this we are not brought into the horizon of

---

[61] So argues Robert Scharlemann in "Shadow on the Tomb," *Dialog,* I (Spring 1962), 22—29.

[62] André Malet concludes his detailed treatment of Bultmann with this analogy (pp. 394—96).

[63] Käsemann, *Exegetische Versuche und Besinnungen,* I, 236.

[64] *Evangelische Evangelienauslegung. Untersuchung zu Luthers Hermeneutik* (1942). Cf. his article, "Die Anfänge von Luthers Hermeneutik," *Zeitschrift für Theologie und Kirche,* XLVIII (1951), 172-230. Ebeling is responsible for the article on Luther's theology in the third edition of *Die Religion in Geschichte und Gegenwart,* IV (Tübingen: J. C. B. Mohr, 1960), 495—519.

metaphors. The linguistic use of metaphors has now quite another task with reference to the subject-matter of theology, namely, to bring man into the real situation, where the subject-matter itself occurs. . . . This understanding of language is not defined from the point of view of signification but from the viewpoint of the word-event which must be accounted for and which, in turn, enables such accountability. The hermeneutical result is, therefore, that the very word as such is of hermeneutical importance and is able to illumine, to bring about clarity, and to give life. The hermeneutical task can only consist of the fact that we devote ourselves to the service of the word-event in such a way that the word becomes truly word, and that it occurs as pure word in the fullness of its power. Luther's thesis on the Bible as *sui ipsius interpres* must be understood along this line.[65]

For Ebeling's Luther, then, the hermeneutical focus does not lie in "verbal description" or in "signification," nor is the Scripture objectively Word; rather, in order for the Word to become "truly" Word, we must "devote ourselves to the service of the word-event." Marlé expresses astonishment at how Ebeling has been able to give Luther "an amazing contemporaneity";[66] quite so: in the above passage Luther is practically indistinguishable from his contemporary interpreter.[67]

Says Ebeling at an earlier point in the article from which the above extended passage was quoted: "We can by no means short-circuit the hermeneutics of the Reformation and pass it off

[65] Gerhard Ebeling, "The New Hermeneutics and the Early Luther," *Theology Today*, XXI (April 1964), 45—46.

[66] Marlé p. 80: "une étonnante actualité."

[67] Robert Scharlemann has recently performed a parallel operation on the great Lutheran theologian of classical orthodoxy, Johann Gerhard. In *Thomas Aquinas and John Gerhard* (New Haven: Yale University Press, 1964), Scharlemann characterizes Gerhard's doctrine of Creation as "the dialectic of obedience" and his doctrine of Redemption as "the dialectic of the court." As Ebeling's Luther comes to sound like Ebeling, so Scharlemann's Gerhard speaks the language of Scharlemann. Contrast Edmund Smits, "The Lutheran Theologians of the 17th Century and the Fathers of the Ancient Church," *The Symposium on Seventeenth Century Lutheranism: Selected Papers*, I (St. Louis, Mo.: The Symposium on Seventeenth Century Lutheranism, 1962), 1—31.

as a mere precursor of modern historico-critical hermeneutics."[68] To which we respond with a hearty "Amen"! Therefore let us by analysis of primary sources determine what in fact Luther's attitude was toward the interpretation of the Biblical text. Is he properly to be aligned with the contemporary dialectical-existential approach, or does he view the Scripture in another way?

The issue here is emphatically not whether Luther's own existential experiences (his realization of justification by grace through faith, his *Anfechtungen*, etc.) played a role in his Biblical exegesis. Certainly they did — as they do for all readers of God's Word. The question is rather whether Luther considered his experiences to conjoin with the Scriptural text in a dialectic manner so that, in the terms of the contemporary hermeneutical circle, each could legitimately work upon the other, and "God's Word could truly become God's Word." Granted that psychological or sociological conditions often led the sensitive Luther to an interest in certain passages of Holy Writ; granted even that on occasion his existential stance colored the Scripture he was endeavoring to understand. But *in principle* did he consider such "word-event" situations to be self-validating, or did he believe that Scripture properly stood over his existential life as an objectively inerrant revelation, proclaiming factual truth to him in judgment and in grace?

Further, the issue of Luther vis-à-vis contemporary hermeneutics does not turn on his employment of Christological exegesis or of the justification principle or of the basic Law-Gospel distinction. That Luther uses these interpretive approaches to Scripture (and sometimes even over-uses them!) no one acquainted with the Reformer's exegetical writings will deny. But this does not commit Luther to a dialectic, experiential hermeneutic. It would do so only if Luther saw these principles as legitimately arising out of existential experience. Does he? Or does he believe that they arise solely from the objective, perspicuous text of an infallible Scripture?

One could attempt to answer these key questions by *catenae* of Luther quotations, derived from the overwhelming riches of the Weimar Ausgabe. But in order to avoid the damning epithet of "prooftexter" and in order to see the issues in the historical context of Luther's life, we shall observe how he employed Scripture in the three major theological controversies of his career: his battle with Roman Catholic ecclesiocentrism, with Erasmian humanism, and with Zwinglian sacramentarianism.

---

[68] Ebeling, "The New Hermeneutics and the Early Luther," p. 35.

At Worms Luther was presented with clean-cut alternatives: recanting his position, which patently ran counter to the *de facto* (shall we say existential?) church teaching of his day, or suffer the ban of the Holy Roman Empire. Not an easy choice. A coward would have recanted; a *hybris*-motivated man would have set the power of his personal existential experience over against the tradition of the church. Luther was neither; his refusal to compromise truth showed that he was no coward, and the total subjection of his existential decision to the Word of Scripture evidenced his humility. Listen to his confession:

> Unless I am convinced by the testimonies of the Holy Scriptures or evident reason (for I believe in neither the Pope nor councils alone, since it has been established that they have often erred and contradicted themselves), I am bound by the Scriptures that I have adduced, and my conscience has been taken captive by the Word of God; and I am neither able nor willing to recant, since it is neither safe nor right to act against conscience. God help me. Amen.[69]

This earth-shaking testimony has become so familiar to us that we neglect to see what precisely it says. If no other statement from Luther were available, his confession at Worms would be sufficient to establish his hermeneutical stance in contradistinction to the current dialectic movement. For Luther says: (1) My conscience — my existential life — has been taken captive by the Word (here clearly identified with the Holy Scriptures); thus Luther, even at the most formidable καιρός of his life, refused to succumb to the temptation of placing personal experience on the same level as God's Word or of giving it any kind of dialectic relation with Scripture (thereby allowing it to become a legitimate basis for his theological stand). (2) The testimonies of the Holy Scriptures are sure — unlike Pope and councils who err and contradict themselves; thus for Luther the objectively inerrant, noncontradictory character of Scripture was taken for granted, in diametric contrast to the objectively fallible judgments of the church. (3) Evident reason is legitimately to be employed in reaching theological truth; thus Luther was no sub-

---

[69] *D. Martin Luthers Werke*, 7, (Weimar: Hermann Böhlaus Nachfolger, 1897), 836—38; hereafter cited as *WA*. See Gordon Rupp's excellent treatment of this incident: *Luther's Progress to the Diet of Worms*, 2d ed. (New York: Harper Torchbooks, 1964), pp. 96 ff.

jectivistic irrationalist who in existential fashion considers an objective, propositionally perspicuous Bible to be an offense to faith.[70]

Indeed, in Luther's Biblical opposition to the Roman Catholicism of his day, we can see exactly the opposite proportion to that suggested by Quanbeck.[71]

Instead of

$$\frac{\text{Medieval exegesis}}{\text{Luther's exegesis}} = \frac{\text{Orthodox hermeneutics}}{\text{Contemporary hermeneutics}}$$

we have

$$\frac{\text{Medieval exegesis}}{\text{Luther's exegesis}} = \frac{\text{Contemporary hermeneutics}}{\text{Orthodox hermeneutics}}$$

Why? Because the Romanism Luther so vehemently opposed consciously permitted a dialectic interrelation between Scripture and existential situation, thereby allowing the latter to influence the interpretation of the former. Beryl Smalley, the foremost specialist on medieval Biblical scholarship, has made clear how, during its formative period, medieval exegesis allowed "present needs" to swallow up the objective message of Scripture:

> The Latin Fathers, followed by the assistants of Charlemagne, made Bible study serve their present needs. They retained both the literal sense and textual criticism, but only as a basis for the spiritual interpretation. First and foremost the Scriptures were a means to holiness. *Lectio divina* formed one side of the ascetic triangle: reading, prayer, contemplation. Equally vital was its role in upholding the faith. The long line of commentators who developed the spiritual senses were not only contemplatives but men of action. They built up the Church, defending her doctrines against pagans, Jews

[70] The ghost of this perennial stereotype of "Luther the existential irrationalist" has been well laid by two recent publications: Robert H. Fischer, "A Reasonable Luther," in *Reformation Studies: Essays in Honor of Roland H. Bainton*, ed. Franklin H. Littell (Richmond, Va.: John Knox Press, 1962), pp. 30—45, 255—56; and B. A. Gerrish, *Grace and Reason: A Study in the Theology of Luther* (Oxford: Clarendon Press, 1962).

[71] See above, the text quotation corresponding to note 59.

and heretics. They rallied to the defense of the Christian State under Charlemagne. They supported the Gregorian reform against the secular power. They set forth the duties of clergy and laity.

They subordinated scholarship meanwhile to mysticism and to propaganda. It was natural in troubled times, when chroniclers were beginning their paragraphs not 'Eo tempore . . .', but 'Ea tempestate. . . .' The decline of biblical scholarship is less surprising than its endurance. The wonder is that even in a minor degree it survived, as a thread, if a slender thread, in the skein that ran from the Alexandrians to the Victorines.[72]

As "early medieval and many twelfth-century commentators had digressed 'anagogically,'" and as the 13th century displayed a "growing interest in things present," so Smalley predicts that in the exegesis of the later Middle Ages "secular interests and naturalism will increase."[73] In this prediction Smalley is quite correct. Torrance has recently shown that Thomas Aquinas, whose theological exegesis so deeply colored the thought patterns of the later medieval church, accepted the "hermeneutical circle"[74] and was unaware of the degree to which he allowed

---

[72] Beryl Smalley, *The Study of the Bible in the Middle Ages* (Oxford: Blackwell, 1952), p. 358.

[73] Ibid., pp. 372—73. On the wide influence of the "fourfold" scheme of Biblical interpretation on medieval exegesis see Harry Caplan, "The Four Senses of Scriptural Interpretation and the Mediaeval Theory of Preaching," *Speculum,* IV (1929), 282—90.

[74] For primary evidence, see *Summa Theol.,* 2.2, q.8, a.1, ad 2; and see T. F. Torrance, "Scientific Hermeneutics According to St. Thomas Aquinas," *The Journal of Theological Studies,* XIII (Oct. 1962), 287—88. Unhappily, Torrance does not see that when church tradition submerges the Biblical text in Thomas' hermeneutic, this is due not to "deficiencies" in his application of the hermeneutical circle but to the very nature of the circle itself, wherein text and interpreter are placed in dialectical relation to each other. A valuable contrast with Thomas' exegesis is provided by the objectively textual approach of Athanasius, who was so highly regarded both by Luther (see Gustaf Aulén, *Christus Victor: An Historical Study of the Three Main Types of the Atonement,* trans. A. G. Hebert [London: SPCK, 1931]) and by the theologians of classical Lutheran orthodoxy (see David Chytraeus, *On Sacrifice: A Reformation Treatise in Biblical Theology,* trans. and ed. John Warwick Montgomery [St. Louis: Concordia Publishing House, 1962]); see T. E. Pollard, "The Exegesis of Scripture and the Arian Controversy," *Bulletin of the John Rylands Library,* XLI (1958—1959), 414—29.

"ecclesiastical tradition" to outweigh the authority of the Scriptural message:

> St. Thomas had a giant mind, to which there have been few equals, but his own immense intellectual powers laid him open to great temptations. His prior understanding of human experience, of the intellect and the soul, his masterful interpretation of Aristotelian physics, metaphysics, and psychology proved too strong and rigid a mould into which to pour the Christian faith. It is philosophy that tends to be the master, while theology tends to lose its unique nature as a science in its own right in spite of the claims advanced for it. In so far as the contents of theology surpass the powers of scientific investigation they are to be accepted as revealed truth but in the end the authority of ecclesiastical tradition outweighs in practice the authority of sacred scripture so that interpretation of revealed truth is schematized to the mind of the church.[75]

The schematization "of revealed truth to the mind of the church" becomes more and more characteristic of Roman Biblical hermeneutics as the medieval period draws to a close, and it reaches a high degree of refinement in such Counter-Reformation interpreters of the Bible as Sixtus of Siena.[76] And it was precisely this existential accommodation of objective Scriptural teaching to "the mind of the church" that Luther opposed at Worms and throughout his career. For him, unlike both medieval Roman and contemporary Protestant hermeneutics,[77] the objective message of God's written Word must stand forever over the corporate and the individual conscience — judging them, not in any sense being judged by them.

---

[75] Torrance, p. 289.

[76] John Warwick Montgomery, "Sixtus of Siena and Roman Catholic Biblical Scholarship in the Reformation Period," *Archiv für Reformationsgeschichte*, LIV/2 (1963), 214—34, now published in the author's *Ecumenicity, Evangelicals, and Rome* (Grand Rapids, Mich.: Zondervan, 1969), chap. ii.

[77] Present-day Roman Catholic scholars, it is worth noting, are exceedingly pleased to see the Protestant move toward dialectic Scriptural interpretation, for such a move opens up the possibility that Protestants, in accepting as legitimate the dynamic force of church tradition in interpreting

Likewise in dealing with the Renaissance humanists of his day Luther stood firm: Scripture speaks as clearly against the ability of the human will in salvation as it does against any form of traditional work-righteousness. Luther's opposition to Erasmus was squarely based on his convictions that whenever Scripture speaks it speaks with absolute authority and clarity, that propositional assertions of truth can, and must, be drawn from the Biblical revelation, and that the literal meaning of the Scriptural text must be accepted unless the Biblical context itself (not any external influence) forces a metaphorical interpretation. Listen to the following typical passages from *De servo arbitrio*, which expressly spell out the distance separating Luther from the nonpropositional, existentially oriented hermeneutics of contemporary Protestantism:

> If you [Erasmus] are referring to essential truths — why, what more irreligious assertion could a man possibly make than that he wants to be free to assert precisely *nothing* about such things? The Christian will rather say this: "So little do I like sceptical principles, that, so far as the weakness of my flesh permits, not merely shall I make it my invariable rule steadfastly to adhere to the sacred text in all that it teaches, and to assert that teaching, but I also want to be as positive as I can about those non-essentials which Scripture does not determine; for uncertainty is the most miserable thing in the world."
> . . . What is this new-fangled religion of yours,

the Bible, will once again listen to the voice of Rome. Readers may be interested in comparing with the earlier-cited contemporary Lutheran approaches to Scripture, "New Shape," Roman Catholic Eduard Schillebeeckx's paper, "Exegesis, Dogmatics and the Development of Dogma," which begins: "The religion of revelation is essentially a dialogue, a meeting between man and the living God," and which sees Christian doctrine as dynamically drawn by the church from the Scriptural *sensus plenior*, not as "formerly theological deductions from New Testament data" (*Dogmatic vs. Biblical Theology*, ed. Herbert Vorgrimler [London: Burns & Oates, 1964], pp. 115—45). Cf. also Lutheran Wilhelm H. Wuellner's unpublished doctoral dissertation, "The Word of God and the Church of Christ: The Ecumenical Implications of Biblical Hermeneutics" (University of Chicago Divinity School, 1958); and for a different evaluation John Warwick Montgomery, "Evangelical Unity in the Light of Contemporary Orthodox Eastern — Roman Catholic — Protestant Ecumenicity," *The Springfielder*, XXX (Autumn 1965), 8—30, now published in the author's *Ecumenicity, Evangelicals, and Rome*, chap. i (see n. 76 above).

this novel sort of humility, that, by your own
example, you would take from us power to
judge men's decisions and make us defer un-
critically to human authority?   Where does
God's written Word tell us to do that?[78]

The notion that in Scripture some things are rec-
ondite and all is not plain was spread by the god-
less Sophists (whom now you echo, Erasmus)
— who have never yet cited a single item to
prove their crazy view; nor can they. And Satan
has used these unsubstantial spectres to scare
men off reading the sacred text, and to destroy
all sense of its value, so as to ensure that his
own brand of poisonous philosophy reigns supreme in the church. I certainly grant that many
passages in the Scriptures are obscure and hard
to elucidate, but that is due, not to the exalted
nature of their subject, but to our own linguistic
and grammatical ignorance. . . . Who will maintain that the town fountain does not stand in
the light because the people down some alley
cannot see it, while everyone in the square can
see it?[79]

Let this be our conviction: that no "implication" or "figure" may be allowed to exist in
any passage of Scripture unless such be required by some obvious feature of the words and
the absurdity of their plain sense, as offending
against an article of faith. Everywhere we should
stick to just the simple, natural meaning of the
words, as yielded by the rules of grammar and
the habits of speech that God has created among
men; for if anyone may devise "implications"
and "figures" in Scripture at his own pleasure,
what will all Scripture be but a reed shaken
with the wind, and a sort of chameleon? There
would then be no article of faith about which
anything could be settled and proved for certain, without your being able to raise objections
by means of some "figure." All "figures" should

---

[78] Martin Luther, *De servo arbitrio, WA,* 18, 604—605.
[79] Ibid., 606.

> rather be avoided, as being the quickest poison,
> when Scripture itself does not absolutely re-
> quire them.[80]

The objective, propositional reliability and clarity of the
Biblical text was also Luther's fundamental hermeneutic assumption in his battles with the sacramentarians over the Real Presence of Christ's body and blood. Here — on what has always
been one of the key points of Lutheran doctrine — the lines are
most decisively drawn between Luther and the modern Protestant hermeneutics. For Luther is so convinced of the verbal
soundness and objective perspicuity of the original text of the
Bible that he is willing to center his whole defense of his Lord's
Supper doctrine on the five words τοῦτό ἐστιν τὸ σῶμά μου. His
book, *That These Words of Christ, "This Is My Body," etc.,
Still Stand Firm Against the Fanatics,* begins with a penetrating
historical survey of the devil's successes in destroying the clear
testimony of the church through corrupting the interpretation
of the Bible. In the Middle Ages, Satan "had some of his followers in the Christians' schools, and through them he stealthily
sneaked and crept into the holy Scriptures"; then Scripture became "like a broken net and no one would be restrained by it, but
everyone made a hole in it wherever it pleased him to poke his
snout, and followed his own opinions, interpreting and twisting
Scripture any way he pleased."[81] And now, says Luther, even
with the restoration of the Gospel and the Scriptures, the
Schwärmer perverts God's Word by refusing to stand under the
literal force of its eucharistic message; again and again Luther
comes back to this same argument — the words of Scripture
must be taken as simple and literal truth:

> Here let the judge between us be not alone
> Christians but also heathen, Turks, Tartars,
> Jews, idolaters, and the whole world: whose re-
> sponsibility is it to prove his text? Should it be
> the Luther who asserts that Moses says, "In the
> beginning the cuckoo ate the hedge sparrow," or
> the person who asserts that Moses says, "In

---

[80] Ibid., 700—701.

[81] Martin Luther, "That These Words of Christ, 'This Is My Body,' etc.,
Still Stand Firm Against the Fanatics," in *Word and Sacrament III*, ed.
Robert H. Fischer, Vol. XXXVII in *Luther's Works*, American Edition, ed.
Jaroslav Pelikan and Helmut T. Lehmann (Philadelphia: Fortress Press,
1961), pp. 13—14.

the beginning God created the heavens and the earth"? I hope the decision would be that Luther ought to prove his text, since in no language does "God" mean the same as "cuckoo." Well, away creeps Luther to the cross, grieved that he cannot prove that "God" means "cuckoo." For anyone who ventures to interpret words in the Scriptures any other way than what they say, is under obligation to prove this contention out of the text of the very same passage or by an article of faith. But who will enable the fanatics to prove that "body" is the equivalent of "sign of the body," and "is" the equivalent of "represents"? No one has brought them to this point up to now.[82]

Luther's encounters with tradition-oriented Romanists, rationalistically inclined humanists, and spiritualistic Protestants leave no doubt as to his standard of religious authority, the degree to which he subjected himself to it, or his approach to its interpretation. For Luther the canonical[83] Scripture was in its entirety God's inerrant Word, and its clear propositional teachings stood in judgment over all other writings. Thus one does not have to look far in Luther to discover such unqualified assertions as the following:

I have learned to ascribe the honor of infallibility only to those books that are accepted as canonical. I am profoundly convinced that none of these writers has erred. All other writers, how-

---

[82] Ibid., p. 32. "His [Luther's] exegesis sought to derive the teachings of the Scriptures from the particular statements of the Scriptures rather than from the *a priori* principles of a theological system. Not even to his own theological speculation, therefore, would Luther consciously accord the status of an *a priori* principle that would dictate his exegesis, even though it cannot be denied that in his exegetical practice he sometimes operated with such *a priori* principles. Hence he was unwilling to have his doctrine of the ubiquity of the body of Christ, which was compounded of exegetical and speculative elements, lay down the terms for his exegesis of 'This is My Body'" (Jaroslav Pelikan, *Luther the Expositor,* companion volume to *Luther's Works,* American Edition [St. Louis, Mo.: Concordia Publishing House, 1959], p. 141).

[83] It should be unnecessary to mention that Luther's early rejection of the General Epistle of James and some other Scripture portions stemmed from his (fallacious) criterion of *canonicity,* not from any weakness in his doctrine of *inspiration.*

ever they may have distinguished themselves in
holiness or in doctrine, I read in this way: I
evaluate what they say, not on the basis that
they themselves believe that a thing is true, but
only insofar as they are able to convince me by
the authority of the canonical books or by clear
reason.[84]

The Holy Scriptures are assuredly clearer, easier
of interpretation, and more certain than any
other writings, for all teachers prove their statements by them, as by clearer and more stable
writings, and wish their own treatises to be established and explained by them. But no one
can ever prove a dark saying by one that is still
darker. Therefore, necessity compels us to run
to the Bible with all the writings of the doctors,
and thence to get our verdict and judgment
upon them; for Scripture alone is the true over-
lord and master of all writings and doctrines on
earth. If not, what are the Scriptures good for?
Lets us reject them and be satisfied with the
books of men and human teachers.[85]

And here we arrive — in language no less than in substantive
content — to the confessional statements of Lutheranism, where
we read:

Luther explicitly made this distinction between
divine and human writings: God's Word alone
is and should remain the only standard and

---

[84] "Defense Against the Ill-tempered Judgment of Eck," WA, 2, 618. This
passage and many others like it demonstrate, as I have argued elsewhere,
that unless we make the clumsy blunder of equating "verbal inspiration"
with traditional Romanist mechanical inspiration (the "dictation theory"),
"it is difficult to feel . . . that Luther, if he lived today, would not in fact
consider 'verbal inspiration' the Biblical view most congenial to his own"
(review of Luther and the Bible by Willem Jan Kooiman, Christianity Today, VI [Feb. 16, 1962], 498).

[85] "An Argument in Defense of All the Articles of Dr. Martin Luther
Wrongly Condemned in the Roman Bull," WA, 7, 308 ff. In the preceding
paragraph of this work Luther asserts his belief that the Scriptures "never
yet have erred" and quotes Augustine as holding the same conviction. Two
excellent treatments of Luther's Scriptural position that reinforce the case
we have been presenting are Lewis W. Spitz, Sr., "Luther's Sola Scriptura,"
Concordia Theological Monthly, XXXI (Dec. 1960) 740—45; and Douglas
Carter, "Luther As Exegete," Concordia Theological Monthly, XXXII
(Sept. 1961), 517—25.

norm of all teachings, and no human being's writings dare be put on par with it, but everything must be subjected to it.[86]

The Lutheran Confessions, then, in harmony with and in dependence on Luther himself, categorically refuse to allow "dialectic relations" between Scripture and any human teacher or writing whatever; the Bible judges man's total existential life — it is not intertwined with it in "hermeneutical circle" or "word-event."[87] Moreover, as Luther derived his Christological theme ("the whole Scripture is about Christ alone everywhere")[88] from Scripture itself, so the Lutheran Confessions ground their justification principle in a verbally perspicuous and totally authoritative Scripture:

> It is surely amazing that our opponents are unmoved by the many passages in the Scriptures that clearly attribute justification to faith and specifically deny it to works. Do they suppose that this is repeated so often for no reason? Do they suppose that these words fell from the Holy Spirit unawares?[89]

---

[86] FC SD, Summary Formulation, 9: "Hoc discrimen (inter divina et humana scripta) perspicue posuit, solas videlicet sacras litteras pro unica regula et norma omnium dogmatum agnoscendas, iisque nullius omnino hominis scripta adaequanda, sed potius omnia subiicienda esse."

[87] Emile Léonard properly interprets Art. V of the Augsburg Confession with this understanding: "Il est bien vrai que, parmi les spiritualistes, Sébastien Franck professait que la Parole agit *ohne Mittel,* sans instrument, et que Schwenckfeld soutenait une doctrine semblable dans son traité *Vom Lauf des Wortes Gottes* (1527). Mais la pointe de l'article était autant contre le catholicisme, avec sa conception d'un Saint-Esprit (incarné dans l'Eglise) indépendant du texte de la Parole" (*Histoire Générale du Protestantisme,* I [Paris: Presses Universitaires de France, 1961], 158).

[88] Luther, *Vorlesung über den Römerbrief, 1515—16,* ed. J. Ficker (4th ed.; Leipzig, 1930), p. 240. Philip S. Watson in lectures on "The Theology of *Sola Scriptura*" (Chicago Lutheran Theological Seminary, Summer 1961) defended Luther's Christological reading of the Old Testament by noting that an entire play can properly be read in terms of its final act; this is quite true, but it should be stressed that Luther could *legitimately* do this (while many modern theologians cannot) because he was fully convinced that the entire Bible is the work of a single "Playwright," whose perspicuous composition warrants such interpretation. For a typical attempt by a contemporary mediating theologian to maintain a Christological view of the Bible, see Nels F. S. Ferré, "Notes by a Theologian on Biblical Hermeneutics," *Journal of Biblical Literature,* LXXVIII (1959), 105—14, and Howard M. Teeple's devastating critique: "Notes on Theologians' Approach to the Bible," *Journal of Biblical Literature,* LXXIX (1960), 164—66.

[89] Ap. IV 107 f.

Never do the Confessions view the central doctrine of justification as arising independently of Scripture or from an existential "life relation" with Scripture — nor do they ever (in accord with a reprehensible modern practice) employ the doctrine as a means of devaluating the literal truth of some portions of Scripture. To the contrary, they recognize full well that apart from the perspicuously inscripturated "words of the Holy Spirit" the fundamental Christian truth of justification could not be sustained at all.

A PERPLEX IN PERSPECTIVE

The hermeneutic of Luther and of the Lutheran Confessions stands, then, in irreconcilable opposition to the existential-dialectic hermeneutic of contemporary Protestant theology. To make of Luther a forerunner of Bultmann — or of Ebeling, Fuchs, or Ott — is almost ludicrous. As I have written elsewhere of the Luther-Bultmann analogy:

> The parallel is, of course, fallacious and "constructed" (cf. the old saw: What does an elephant and a tube of toothpaste have in common? Answer: Neither one can ride a bicycle). Whereas Luther turned from moral guilt to confidence in the *objective* facts of Christ's death for his sin and resurrection for his justification, Bultmann turns from his intellectual doubts to *subjective* anthropological salvation — a direct about-face from the objective Gospel Luther proclaimed.[90]

The contemporary hermeneutic is, as we have seen, a re-pristination of the very approach to the Bible Luther opposed throughout his career. Luther constantly strove to maintain the objective purity of the Biblical message over against all adulterations of God's Word with human opinions. Existential-dialectic approaches to Scripture invariably produce such adulterations, for by interlocking text and interpreter into a "word-event" relationship uncontrolled by the subject-object distinction, they permit — if they do not actually encourage — the absorption of the Scriptural teaching into the existential-cultural situation of the interpreter. Instead of God's Word re-creating man in God's image, man re-creates God's Word in his own image.

[90] John Warwick Montgomery, *The Shape of the Past: An Introduction to Philosophical Historiography* (Ann Arbor, Mich.: Edwards, 1963), pp. 159—60.

Commenting on the Second Drew University Consultation on Hermeneutics, which so well reflects today's perplex in Biblical interpretations, Robert Funk, perceptively wrote:

> Neo-orthodoxy taught that God is never object but always subject, with the result that third generation neo-orthodox theologians have been forced to wrestle with the non-phenomenal character of God. They are unwilling to settle for God as noumenon (perhaps as a legacy of theologies of history, and perhaps as the result of a radical empiricism), which means that for them God does not "appear" at all. . . .

> It is possible on this circumspective view to see why the question of non-objectifying speaking and thinking in theology is a crucial problem, and yet why it refuses to come into focus: it touches upon a root question, viz., can or how can one speak meaningfully of God, but it is also difficult to address in an ordered and logical way because it is not apparent what "logic" is appropriate to the question.[91]

Here the chasm between Luther and the 20th-century hermeneutic yawns the widest, for Luther was never in doubt as to the "logic" appropriate to divine-human communication: It was and would always remain the logic of the Scriptural address. For Luther and for confessional Lutheranism, over against the *finitum non capax infiniti* tradition common both to idealistic philosophy and to classical Calvinism, God is indeed capable of "appearing" in the human situation and of making His will known to man in univocal language. When the contemporary hermeneutic reaches the nadir of "non-objectifying speaking and thinking in theology," it simply betrays its refusal to accept what for Luther was axiomatic to all theology: God is able to speak absolute, objective truth to man in man's language, and the Bible is that inerrant discourse. Luther's Christological principle in Biblical hermeneutics has implications few modern Lutherans wish to face; for just as Luther refused to limit the Incarnation or the Real Presence through rational speculation about what God could or could not do, so he would have had no patience with our endeavors to limit revelation to God's "acts" (as distinguished from His

---

[91] Funk, pp. 303—304.

Scriptural words), to the "doctrinal" content of Scripture (over against its "non-theological" material), or to the "spiritual" in the Bible. The God of Luther and of confessional Lutheranism has never been tongue-tied.

The 20th-century hermeneutic perplex in theology is a reflection of the general cultural confusion of the epoch. Smalley, it will be remembered,[92] commented that the decline of medieval hermeneutics "was natural in troubled times." Certainly we today begin our chronicles with *Ea tempestate*, and the chaos of hot and cold wars has unsettled us to the point where subjective relativism — the bias against the objective absolutes — has come to dominate even the field of theology, where there is least justification for it.[93]

Ironically, nontheological disciplines have in recent years been far more successful than theology in recovering ground lost to "nonobjectivistic" thinking. In spite of the popular view that Einsteinian physics and Heisenberg's Indeterminacy Principle have obliterated the subject-object distinction in favor of an "existential dynamism" in science, "Bohr has emphasized the fact that the observer and his instruments must be presupposed in any investigation, so that the instruments are not part of the phenomenon described but are used."[94] In philosophy, the existential tide that has conditioned so much of the twentieth century theology is receding under the impact of powerful analytical and linguistic criticism which has shown that dialectic-existential affirmations, owing to their subjective non-testability, are technically meaningless.[95] How remarkably like a modern philosophical-linguistic analyst is Luther when he says that he should send the nonpropositional Erasmus off to Anticyra — a health resort

---

[92] See above, the text quotation corresponding to note 72.

[93] See John Warwick Montgomery, "Ascension Perspective," *The Cresset*, XXIV (May 1961), 17—19.

[94] Victor F. Lenzen, *Procedures of Empirical Science*, Vol. I, No. 5 in *International Encyclopedia of Unified Science* (Chicago: *University of Chicago Press*, 1938), p. 28.

[95] John Warwick Montgomery, "Inspiration and Inerrancy: A New Departure," (*Evangelical Theological Society Bulletin*, VIII [Spring 1965], 45—75, now published in this author's *Crisis in Lutheran Theology*, Vol. 1 [Grand Rapids, Mich.: Baker, 1967], chap. 1) applies the insights of analytical philosophy to the question of Biblical authority; noninerrancy inspiration claims for the Bible (particularly those by contemporary Lutherans) are there seen to be philosophically nonsensical and theologically at variance with the Biblical epistemology.

for the mentally ill — since Erasmus necessarily *asserts* that he finds *no satisfaction in assertions!*[96]

In the historical field also, the presuppositions of existentialism are being seriously questioned. The Dilthey tradition of subjective historiography (which has so profoundly colored Biblical scholarship from Barth and Bultmann to the post-Bultmannians) is incapable of sustaining the criticisms directed at it by analytically trained philosophers of history. So, for example, J. W. N. Watkins, reflecting the new drive toward objectivity in historical study, has little patience with the idea that "to understand Ghengis Khan the historian must be someone very like Ghengis Khan" and points out that historical truth is determined not by the historian's subjective "temperament and mentality" but by his inductive examination of factually objective evidence.[97]

A recent literary tour de force has particularly well evidenced the growing self-awareness by belletristic scholars of the ghastly results of existential "life relation" thinking in literary criticism. Frederick C. Crews of the English Department at the University of California (Berkeley), in *The Pooh Perplex,* has "analyzed" A. A. Milne's perennial children's classic, *Winnie the Pooh,*[98] through assuming the guise of "several academicians of varying critical persuasions."[99] Here we have a series of hilarious examples of what invariably happens when interpreters create an "existentially dynamic" relation between themselves and their text. "Harvey C. Window," author of a casebook significantly titled, *What Happened at Bethlehem,* writes on the "paradoxical" in Pooh; for him "all great literature is more complex than the naive reader can suspect," the literal meaning is to give way to "multivalent symbolism," and when the events of the book do not fit his paradoxical categories, they are reinterpreted until they do so. "P. R. Honeycomb," a poetical contributor to the

---

[96] *WA,* 18, 603-605.

[97] J. W. N. Watkins, "Philosophy of History: Publications in English," in *La Philosophie au milieu du vingtième siècle,* ed. Raymond Klibansky, 4 vols., 2d ed. (Firenze, 1961—62), III, 159, 174. On the implications of analytical historiography for theology of history, see my concluding chapter, "Toward a Christian Philosophy of History," in Carl F. H. Henry's symposium, *Jesus of Nazareth: Savior and Lord* (Grand Rapids, Mich.: Eerdmans, 1966).

[98] In a theological paper such as this it seems only right to cite the eminent Latin translation of Pooh: *Winnie ille Pu,* trans. Alexander Lenard (Novi Eboraci: Sumptibus Duttonis, 1960).

[99] Frederick C. Crews, *The Pooh Perplex* (New York: Dutton Paperbacks, 1965).

"little magazines" who engages in "intensely personal criticism," brings his existential stance to bear on the text: "In wondering what I shall set down next in these notations, I am reminded of Heisenberg's Uncertainty Principle. The only thing that is certain is that I am uncertain what to set down next, and in this I typify the whole modern age and the collision of elementary particles in particular, a fact I find peculiarly comforting." "Myron Masterson," a distinguished "angry young man" for the past 20 years, writes on "Poisoned Paradise: The Underside of Pooh," employing as his guides Karl Marx, St. John of the Cross, Friedrich Nietzsche, Sacco and Vanzetti, Sigmund Freud, and C. G. Jung; he rejects those finicky "experts" who have said that "there exist differences of opinion among these thinkers," for, after all, "each of them has helped to shape my literary and moral consciousness." "Woodbine Meadowlark," a perpetual graduate student romantically overwhelmed by the *Angst* of existence, paints a poohological picture in exact conformity with his world view:

> The most perfect emblem of ignorance is contained in the "Woozle" scene, which gives us Pooh and Piglet (ethereal, pure-hearted Piglet, the real hero of the book) wandering helplessly in circles, following their own darling little tracks and misconceiving their goal ever more thoroughly as they proceed. Is this not the very essence of modern man, aching with existential *nausée* and losing himself more deeply in despair as his longing for certainty waxes?

"Simon Lacerous," editor of the feared quarterly, *Thumbscrew,* describes Pooh as "Another Book to Cross Off Your List" and terminates his acid analysis by completely losing the subject-object distinction between the book and himself; indeed, to use Fuchs' terminology (but hardly in a manner to please Fuchs), the poohological word has "objectified" its interpreter: "The more I think about it, the more convinced I become that Christopher Robin not only hates everything I stand for, he hates me personally." Finally, "Smedley Force," a spokesman for "responsible criticism," completely submerges the text by his interest in literary antecedents, conjectural emendations, and the "discovery" of errors and inconsistencies in the book. Such endeavors, he is convinced, place us "on the threshold of the Golden Age of POOH!"[100]

The fervent desire to avoid just such a "golden age of Pooh" has led more and more literary critics to stop running in hermeneutical circles (the *Doppeldeutigkeit* is intentional) and to seek objective canons of interpretation. The result can be seen in such a superlative study as Elder Olson's "Hamlet and the Hermeneutics of Drama,"[101] where, over against all existential blendings of text and interpreter, Olson defines a perfect interpretation as "one which is absolutely commensurate in its basic, inferential, and evaluative propositions with the data, the implications, and the values contained within the work." Theologians should carefully ponder Olson's essay, for, just as he notes that the only alternative to this objective approach is "an endless succession of free improvisations on Shakespearean themes," so modern theology has offered ample evidence that the dialectic hermeneutic yields but a parallel series of unrestrained improvisations on God's Word.

Even in the theological field (where an oddly conservative temperament seems to encourage the persistence of liberal folly long after it has been rejected in other areas of knowledge!) there is evidence that hermeneutics is awaking from an enchanted sleep of half a century. Thus, as we have seen earlier,[102] Cullmann has disengaged himself from Barth's "theological exegesis." More significant yet is James Barr's demonstration that the dialectic "revelation through history" approach of the Neo-Orthodox "Biblical theology movement" has colored with theological *a priori* even such an ostensibly reliable work as Kittel's *Wörterbuch*. Albrecht Oepke, who in the *Wörterbuch* claims that "revelation is not the communication of rational knowledge,"[103] is taken by Barr as "a very bad example" of the absorption of philology by modern theological presuppositionalism.[104] In his inaugural ad-

---

[100] The book also provides samples of Marxist and psychoanalytic interpretations of Pooh and some fascinating literary analyses based on specialized hermeneutic principles.

[101] Elder Olson, "Hamlet and the Hermeneutics of Drama," *Modern Philology,* LXI (Feb. 1964), 225—37.

[102] Note 19 above and corresponding text.

[103] Albrecht Oepke, ἀποκαλύπτω *Theologisches Wörterbuch zum Neuen Testament,* ed. Gerhard Kittel, III (Stuttgart: Verlag von W. Kohlhammer, 1938), 575.

[104] Barr shows that Oepke's article "is assimilated to modern theological usage to a degree that the actual linguistic material will not bear" (James Barr, *The Semantics of Biblical Language* [London: Oxford University Press, 1961], p. 230).

dress at Princeton in December 1962 Barr drew the lines even sharper.

> God can speak specific verbal messages, when he wills, to the men of his choice. But for this, if we follow the way in which the Old Testament represents the incidents, there would have been no call of Abraham, no Exodus, no prophecy. Direct communication from God to man has fully as much claim to be called the core of the tradition as has revelation through events in history. If we persist in saying that this direct, specific communication must be subsumed under revelation through events in history and taken as subsidiary interpretation of the latter, I shall say that we are abandoning the Bible's own representation of the matter.[105]

From philosophical theology severe criticisms are beginning to be voiced against the epistemological sloppiness of existentially immediate truth claims and against the strangely illogical argument, so frequently heard today, that to expect any kind of objective grounding for Christian affirmations is to exhibit unfaith.[106]

In short, the hermeneutic of Luther and of the Lutheran Confessions can hardly be regarded as obscurantist today. In its insistence that "sensus literalis sive historicus . . . solus tota est fidei et theologiae Christianae substantia,"[107] it stands with the most advanced and clearheaded of contemporary scholarship.

But a far more powerful reason than scholarship *per se* impels us to hold on to the Lutheran hermeneutic. We have seen that the central doctrines of the Lutheran faith, such as justification and the Real Presence, were derived from Scripture through the application of this hermeneutic. To the extent that we move away from the literal sense and plain meaning of Scripture, to that very extent we undermine the salvatory doctrines Scripture

---

[105] James Barr, "The Interpretation of Scripture. II. Revelation Through History in the Old Testament and in Modern Theology," *Interpretation,* XVII (April 1963), 201—202.

[106] See, for example, Frederick Ferré, *Language, Logic and God* (New York: Harper & Row, 1961), especially pp. 94—104; and several papers in *New Essays in Philosophical Theology,* ed. Antony Flew and Alasdair MacIntyre (London: SCM Press, 1955), especially C. B. Martin, "A Religious Way of Knowing" (pp. 76—95), and Ronald W. Hepburn, "Demythologizing and the Problem of Validity." (pp. 227—42)

[107] *WA,* 14, 560.

proclaims and our church has so courageously preached. Desertion of the Lutheran hermeneutic by the introduction of non-verbal, nonpropositional, noninerrant conceptions of the Bible is, though we may not wish to see it, the ancient Calvinist *finitum non capax infiniti* heresy rearing its head;[108] and the result will be the eventual loss of the Real Presence and possibly even (as in Calvinistic modernism) the disappearance of any genuine Incarnation.[109] To substitute a dialectic-existential "event of interpretation" for the objective message of *sola Scriptura* is to fall back into the subjectivistic evils of Pietism, to which more than one critic of Bultmann has attributed his theological failings.[110]

Moreover, let us not deceive ourselves into thinking that hermeneutics and Biblical inspiration are distinct problems or that hermeneutical decisions have no necessary bearing on our doctrine of inspiration. A few years ago an exceedingly important paper was published with the title "Hermeneutics as a Cloak for the Denial of Scripture";[111] in it the author demonstrated by example how a non-literal, nonobjective hermeneutic can sap the meaning out of Scripture so as actually to deny its inspiration. Whenever we reach the point of affirming on the one hand that the Bible is infallible or inerrant and admitting on the other hand to internal contradictions or factual inaccuracies within it, we not only make a farce of language, promoting ambiguity, confusion, and perhaps even deception in the church; more reprehensible than even these things, we in fact deny the plenary inspiration and authority of Scripture, regardless of the theological formulae we may insist on retaining.

And if church history can teach us anything, it should teach us that seemingly minute problems of Biblical hermeneutics (such as the historicity of Jonah and the leviathan) never remain minute. The decisions made on the "small" problems govern subsequent decisions on larger issues. Scripture is a seamless garment, and when the threads are unraveled at one place,

---

[108] So John R. Lavik criticizes Joseph Sittler's dialectic view of inspiration (*The Christian Church in a Secularized World* [Minneapolis: Augsburg, 1952], pp. 72—73).

[109] This should be carefully observed especially by those who assert that the hermeneutic of propositional inerrancy deserves the pejorative epithet "Calvinist-fundamentalist."

[110] See, e.g., Reginald H. Fuller, *The New Testament in Current Study*, rev. ed. (London: SCM Press, 1963), p. 30.

[111] J. Barton Payne, "Hermeneutics as a Cloak for the Denial of Scripture," *Evangelical Theological Society Bulletin*, III (Fall 1960), 93—100.

soon the entire fabric gives away. From Jonah to the Resurrection is as short a distance as our Lord Himself placed between them.

Permissiveness in regard to the basic hermeneutic of Lutheranism is the surest way of introducing permissiveness throughout the entire doctrinal spectrum. Why? Because all doctrine (and this includes the contents of the creeds and confessions) derives from Scripture, and vagueness in Biblical interpretation will most definitely yield, sooner or later, vagueness in the understanding of confessional teaching.[112] Let us not soon forget this fact, for more powerful churches than ours have in an unbelievably short time and in our own experience passed doctrinally into a "golden age of Pooh" through hermeneutic contamination.

And if, having reached the end of this somewhat involved essay, we hesitate in our commitment to Luther's hermeneutic of literal sense and objective perspicuity, doubtless we can benefit from some maieutic advice. First let us hear from Luther as he stresses the eschatological merit of his hermeneutic as compared with the interpretive approach of the subjectively oriented *Schwärmer*:

> Even supposing that our text and interpretation were uncertain or obscure — which it is not — as well as their text and interpretation, you still have this glorious, reassuring advantage that you can rely upon our text with a good conscience and say, "If I must have an uncertain, obscure text and interpretation, I would rather have the one uttered by the lips of God himself than one uttered by the lips of men. And if I must be deceived, I would rather be deceived by God (if that were possible) than by men. For if God deceives me, he will take the responsibility and make amends to me, but men cannot make amends to me if they have deceived me and led me into hell."[113]

---

[112] Marlé stresses the related point that hermeneutic issues bear directly on interconfessional dialog and ecumenical discussion (pp. 97—102). Here also an unambiguous hermeneutic is mandatory.

[113] Martin Luther, "Confession Concerning Christ's Supper," *Word and Sacrament III*, p. 305.

Finally we shall listen to Gilbert Murray, one of the greatest classicists of our century, who, like Luther, had confidence in words.

> [We must] pause before thinking that it is a simple matter to understand and interpret even a book in our own language and belonging to our own civilization, not to speak of one removed from us by great gulfs.

> And yet, as I said, we do it. It is a question, I suppose, of caring and of taking pains. I am often struck, when I read controversial literature about Homer, say, or Plato, to notice how comparatively small a part of the field the controversy covers. If you take the whole of what Plato or Homer means to one of the disputants, and the whole of what he means to the other, nine-tenths of the two wholes coincide. And they often coincide in the most important and essential things, those which are felt and do not particularly claim to be talked about. In the language of the stage, the great things "carry" — across the footlights, and across the ages.[114]

Perhaps the καιρός has come for Lutherans to take stock of themselves: to see that they do not become enmeshed in a hermeneutic perplex when the interpretive task is, like most profoundly spiritual things, disarmingly simple: to bow to the full authority of God's Word that it may carry across the footlights to our darkling age.

---

[114] Gilbert Murray, *The Interpretation of Ancient Greek Literature; an Inaugural Lecture Delivered Before the University of Oxford, January 27, 1909* (Oxford: Clarendon Press, 1909), p. 18.

II
LUTHER AND SCIENCE

CROSS, CONSTELLATION, AND CRUCIBLE

The Two Revolutions

For most of us, living today in the wake of Marx and Engels' *Communist Manifesto,* the term "revolution" has an inevitably political connotation. For the traditional historian, moreover, schooled in the vicissitudes of national history, such an interpretation is even more to be expected. Thus the "revolutionary period" generally represents either the late eighteenth-century overthrow of English rule in the American colonies and of the Old Régime in France; or the mid-nineteenth century, with its great year of revolutions, 1848; or the Bolshevist success in 1917. But these alterations in the political climate, important as they were, pale in comparison with the radical changes in the total outlook of Western man which occurred in the Europe of the sixteenth and seventeenth centuries.

The years from 1500 to 1700 witnessed not one, but two, staggering revolutions of thought. In cosmology, the Copernican revolution, culminating in the discoveries of Brahe and Kepler, totally changed man's conception of the physical universe. Sir James Jeans, in his historical survey, *The Growth of Physical Science,* properly describes the high years of this period as "the century of genius." Simultaneously with this cosmological revolution came a theological revolution — the Reformation. Not without reason modern Luther scholars such as Heinrich Boehmer, Anders Nygren, and Philip Watson have spoken of Luther's break with the medieval thought-world as a "Copernican revolution in theology." As Watson well puts it: "Just as Copernicus started with a geocentric, but reached a heliocentric conception of the physical world, Luther began with an anthropocentric or egocentric conception of religion, but came to a theocentric conception. In this sense, Luther is a Copernicus in the realm of religion."[1]

The simultaneity of the Copernican and Lutheran revolutions suggests a more than accidental relationship between them. In speaking of these two radical transformations of thought, Heinrich Bornkamm of Heidelberg has argued: "Intellectual revolutions cannot be entirely divorced from one another in the hearts of the same era."[2] And yet just such a divorce is widely maintained today both by historians of culture in general and

---

[1] Philip S. Watson, *Let God Be God! An Interpretation of the Theology of Martin Luther* (London: Epworth Press, 1947), p. 34.

[2] Heinrich Bornkamm, *Luther's World of Thought,* trans. Martin H. Bertram (St. Louis, Mo.: Concordia Publishing House, 1958), p. 177.

by historians of science and of theology in particular. Thus
popular historian-philosopher Will Durant, relying as usual upon
secondary and tertiary sources and upon the *a prioris* of eighteenth-century rationalism, writes:

> Protestantism could not favor science, for it
> based itself on an infallible Bible. Luther re-
> jected the Copernican astronomy because the
> Bible told of Joshua commanding the sun —
> not the earth — to stand still. Melanchthon
> was inclined to science; he studied mathematics,
> physics, astronomy, and medicine, and lectured
> on the history of mathematics in antiquity; but
> his broad spirit was overwhelmed by the forceful
> nature of his master, and by the predominance
> of a narrowed Lutheranism after Luther's death.
> Calvin had little use for science; Knox none.[3]

The same general interpretation is presented in numerous histories of science, such as A. Wolf's *A History of Science, Technology, and Philosophy in the 16th & 17th Centuries*, where one
reads that the Copernican system "was opposed from the beginning by Luther and the Reformers."[4] The roots of this anti-
scientific view of the Lutheran Reformation may well go back to
Erasmus' famous dictum that "Wherever Lutheranism prevails,
there we see the downfall of learning";[5] in any case, the modern
statement of the position derives from such nineteenth-century
Roman Catholic apologists as Franz Beckmann (*Zur Geschichte
des Kopernikanischen Systems*), Franz Hipler (*Nikolaus Ko-
pernicus und Martin Luther*), and Adolf Mueller, S.J. (*Nicolaus
Copernicus*), and from Andrew Dickson White's greatly influential work, *A History of the Warfare of Science with Theology
in Christendom* (wherein, to employ cinematographic terminology, the "good guys" — represented by Science — always win
against the "bad guys" — represented by revealed Religion).[6]

[3] Will Durant, *The Reformation* ("The Story of Civilization," VI; New
York: Simon and Schuster, 1957), p. 849.
[4] A. Wolf, *A History of Science, Technology, and Philosophy in the 16th
& 17th Centuries* (2 vols., 2d ed.; New York: Harper Torchbooks, 1959), I,
25.
[5] Erasmus, *Opus epistolarum*, ed. P. S. Allen *et al.* (12 vols.; Oxford: Clarendon Press, 1906-1958), VII, 366.
[6] It pains me to reveal that White was the first president of my Alma
Mater! Indeed, he writes in his Introduction: "This book is presented as a
sort of *Festschrift* — a tribute to Cornell University as it enters the second
quarter-century of its existence."

Even in positive treatments of the Reformation one finds little to counter the impression that the Lutheran movement was hostile to scientific advance; neither Karl Holl's *Cultural Significance of the Reformation,* nor the recent composite works, *Luther and Culture* (Volume IV of the Martin Luther Lectures series) and *The Church and Modern Culture* (sponsored by the Lutheran Academy for Scholarship), deal with the problem at all.

Indeed, even when a grudging concession is made that the Reformation may have had some beneficial effect on the rise of modern science, the argument has been stated in such terms that Calvinism, and not Lutheranism, receives the credit. The best example of this approach, and certainly the most influential, is the work of the late Ernst Troeltsch, who held that the chief contribution of Protestantism to science lay in the negative consideration that Protestants "destroyed previously existing Church-controlled science, and secularized, at least from a legal point of view, educational institutions";[7] and who maintained the thesis that whereas Calvinism engaged in "the systematic discipline of the senses," finding it "impossible to deny the world in theory and enjoy it in practice," and so indirectly contributed to the empirical activism of modern science, "Lutheranism depreciated this world, mourning over it as a 'vale of tears,' but so far as everything else was concerned the Lutheran, happy in the assurance of justification, and nourished by the Presence of Christ in the sacraments, let things remain as they were."[8] A not entirely dissimilar implication that Lutheran theology, as contrasted with Calvinism, offers an unsatisfactory basis for philosophy of science appears in the most recent article on the subject — titled "The Influence of Reformed Theology on the Development of Scientific Method" — by T. F. Torrance of Edinburgh, a writer nonetheless sympathetic to the Reformation.[9]

In the present essay an attempt will be made to set forth the actual relationship between Lutheranism and science during the Reformation period. This will be done, first, by some preliminary remarks concerning Luther's own attitude toward the natural world and toward the investigation of it, and second, by a detailed study of the hitherto uninvestigated activities of

---

[7] Ernst Troeltsch, *Protestantism and Progress,* trans. W. Montgomery (Boston: Beacon Press Paperbacks, 1958), pp. 155 ff.

[8] Ernst Troeltsch, *The Social Teaching of the Christian Churches,* trans. Olive Wyon (2 vols.; New York: Harper Torchbooks, 1960), II, 606 ff.

[9] T. F. Torrance, "The Influence of Reformed Theology on the Development of Scientific Method," *Dialog,* II (Winter, 1963), 46.

Lutheran astrologers and alchemists of the period, who exemplify in their scientific labors Luther's theological orientation. In the course of our journey into these almost totally neglected by-ways in the history of ideas, we shall perhaps also discover significant insights to aid us in conquering the frightful contemporary dehumanization of science and descientification of the humanities so well pointed up by C. P. Snow in his *Two Cultures*.

LUTHER AND SCIENCE

The alleged opposition between Lutheranism and scientific progress during the Reformation period is, as Will Durant has already illustrated for us, generally argued on the basis of Luther's resistance to the Copernican theory. Now it is quite true that Luther on one occasion set over against the Biblical account of Joshua's commanding the sun to stand still the view of "a certain new astrologer who proved that the earth moves."[10] However, those who confidently quote this passage (usually from a late, redacted text) are invariably unaware that (1) Copernicus is not named in the passage, so it is not absolutely certain that Luther had him in mind; (2) the statement was a conversational table remark made in the year 1539, four years before anything by Copernicus had been printed, and so could not possibly have been made on the basis of an actual study of Copernicus' arguments; (3) this is the only such remark contained in the entire corpus of Luther's writings — extending to some seventy-five volumes in the best critical edition; Luther, in other words, made no negative comments on Copernicus' theory after the publication of the *De revolutionibus* in 1543; (4) Luther elsewhere makes clear that he is quite willing to admit that the Biblical writers can and do describe physical phenomena from their own observational standpoint and not in absolute terms;[11] thus the Joshua passage could not have been for him an insuperable barrier to the acceptance of the Copernican position; and, finally, (5) Luther's one passing remark, which may or may not have been directed to Copernicus, did not appear in print until 1566 — a full twenty years after Luther's death — so it cannot be regarded as having acted as an actual deterrent to the spread

---

[10] *Tischreden* (hereafter cited as *TR*), IV, 4638, in the standard, critical *Weimarer Ausgabe* (hereafter cited as *WA*) of Luther's works.

[11] Luther commented in 1530 on Ps. 24:2: "To this day philosophers debate where the earth stands. Scripture says that it was established on the waters and speaks according to what the eyes see. For the earth is in the waters, so to speak, as Genesis says, 'Let the dry land appear,' which is what we see before our eyes" (*WA*, XXXI, Pt. I, 370).

of the new world picture among Lutherans or others. Indeed,
followers of Luther were instrumental in the initial promotion of
Copernicus' theory. Werner Elert of Erlangen, after an exhaus-
tive study of the problem, wrote:

> It is certain that Copernicus himself was and re-
> mained a faithful son of the Roman Church. But
> no historian will cover up the facts that a Luther-
> an prince [Duke Albrecht of Prussia] sub-
> sidized the publication of his work, that a Lu-
> theran theologian [Andreas Osiander] arranged
> for the printing, and that a Lutheran mathema-
> tician [Joachim Rhaeticus] supervised the
> printing — a Lutheran mathematician who was
> second to none in working for the introduc-
> tion of the new world picture and did not forfeit
> the friendship of Melanchthon by doing so.[12]

As for Melanchthon, Luther's closest reforming associate, who,
according to Durant, was "overwhelmed" by Luther's supposedly
anti-scientific attitude, it is seen that he moved from an initial
resistance to Copernicus to a genuine appreciation for his work;
in 1549 he stated publicly, "We have begun to admire and love
Copernicus more,"[13] and in the second and subsequent editions
of his *Elements of Physics* he dropped all references expressing
antagonism to Copernicus.[14]

But, on the positive side, what in fact was Luther's attitude
toward the natural world and toward the investigation of it?
Was he, as Troeltsch suggests, the spiritual father of quietists
who used the Real Presence of Christ in the Sacrament as a
shield from the earthly "vale of tears"? Such a picture could not
be more contrary to the actual Luther of history. Luther's
sermons and Bible commentaries are replete with illustrations
from the natural world, and he self-consciously contrasts his
evangelical approach in this respect with the attitude of Erasmus
and other humanists:

---

[12] Werner Elert, *The Structure of Lutheranism*, I, trans. Walter A. Hansen
(St. Louis, Mo.: Concordia Publishing House, 1962), p. 423.

[13] *Corpus Reformatorum* (hereafter cited as *CR*), XI, 839.

[14] See Emil Wohlwill "Melanchthon und Copernicus," *Mitteilungen zur
Geschichte der Medizin und der Naturwissenschaften*, III (1904), 260-67;
and cf. Preserved Smith, *The Age of the Reformation* (New York: Henry
Holt, 1920), pp. 621-22.

> We are beginning to regain a knowledge of the
> creation, a knowledge we had forfeited by the
> fall of Adam. Now we have a correct view of
> created reality, more so, I suppose, than they
> have in the papacy. Erasmus does not concern
> himself with this; it interests him little how the
> fetus is made, formed, and developed in the
> womb. Thus he also fails to prize the excellency
> of the state of marriage. But by God's mercy
> we can begin to recognize His wonderful works
> and wonders also in the flowers when we ponder
> His might and His goodness. Therefore we laud,
> magnify, and thank Him. In His creation we
> recognize the power of His Word. By His Word
> everything came into being. This power is evi-
> dent even in a peach stone. No matter how hard
> its shell, in due season it is forced open by a very
> soft kernel inside it. All this is ignored by
> Erasmus. He looks at the creation as a cow
> stares at a new gate.[15]

For Luther, "heaven and earth [are] full of the fire of divine
love, full of life and righteousness, full of glory and praise";[16] in
the last year of his life he wrote in a volume of Pliny's *Natural
History*, "All creation is the most beautiful book or Bible; in it
God has described and portrayed Himself."[17]

These statements by Luther are the key to his view of the
natural world, and show clearly that his positive attitude to the
study of nature grew directly from his central theological insights. For Luther, when God became man in Jesus Christ, the
Word of God (to use the Johannine terminology) did in fact
"become flesh," and thus the entire natural world was hallowed
by God. This hallowing continues, moreover, even after the
Ascension of Christ, for the whole Christ, body and spirit, is
present throughout the universe today. When we speak in the
Creed of Christ sitting on God's right hand, we must realize that
just as God is everywhere, so the God-man Jesus Christ is everywhere, displaying His grace and love. Thus Luther's stress on
the Real Presence in the Eucharist, instead of producing quietism, as Troeltsch claims, produced a vital interest in the natural

[15] *WA — TR*, I, 1160.

[16] *WA*, XX, 229.

[17] *WA*, XLVIII, 201.

world as capable of displaying Christ (for, as the dogmaticians' formula put it, *finitum capax infiniti*, "the finite is capable of the infinite"). In opposition to Roman Catholics, who regarded Christ's Presence in the Sacrament as altering ("transubstantiating") the natural, and in opposition to Calvinists, who separated Christ from the world by asserting the impossibility of His bodily presence everywhere, Luther, and the theological tradition stemming from him, saw the Christ who saves us as "substantially present everywhere, in and through all creatures, in all their parts and places"[18] — "even in the most insignificant leaf of a tree."[19] In consequence, the investigation of the world of nature was, for Luther and his followers, in the final analysis a confrontation with the Christ of the Cross, who forms the center of all true theology. No greater incentive to scientific activity could be imagined.

CROSS AND CONSTELLATION

But did the Lutherans of the Reformation period engage in substantial scientific activity? The standard histories of science can be searched in vain to discover evidence of it. Yet the evidence does exist — in realms normally regarded, by historians of culture and historians of theology, as esoteric and fanciful. Here we enter the domains of astrology and alchemy, and we shall find them of far more than antiquarian curiosity in displaying the Lutheran contribution to science during the Reformation era.

In Lynn Thorndike's massive *History of Magic and Experimental Science,* there is a commonly overlooked chapter entitled, "The Circle of Melanchthon."[20] Here Thorndike sets forth in his usual chronicle-like, non-interpretative fashion, an account of the numerous scholars who studied at Wittenberg under Melanchthon — rightly called "the Preceptor of Germany" — and then carried their learning to the far corners of Europe. One of the chief interests of this Melanchthonian "school" lay in astrology-astronomy. Melanchthon himself was an avid astrologer, as his most recent English biographer, Manschreck, points out.[21] It must be admitted that Melanchthon re-

---

[18] *WA,* XXIII, 134 ff.

[19] *WA,* XXIII, 132.

[20] Lynn Thorndike, *A History of Magic and Experimental Science,* V (New York: Columbia University Press, 1941), 378-405.

[21] Clyde L. Manschreck, *Melanchthon, the Quiet Reformer* (New York: Abingdon Press, 1958), pp. 102-112 and *passim.*

ceived little astrological support from Luther (the latter once remarked that his friend pursued astrology "as I take a drink of strong beer when I am troubled with grievous thoughts"[22]), but Luther held a high opinion of astronomy; "we will gladly allow astronomy," he said on one occasion, "but I cannot bear astrology, because it has no demonstrable proof — its prophecies are so doubtful";[23] and he asserted that "astronomy is the oldest science and has been instrumental in introducing many arts."[24] Of course, astronomy and astrology were thoroughly intertwined in the Melanchthon circle, and may be observed in the work of all of its members.

The positive influence of this Lutheran circle of astrologer-astronomers on the progress of physical science was immense. For one thing, as already noted, it was the Lutherans who did the most to promote the dissemination of Copernicus' ideas. The two chief figures in this activity were Joachim Rhaeticus and Erasmus Reinhold, both professors at Wittenberg and prominent members of the Melanchthon circle. Rhaeticus, as we have seen, supervised the printing of the first edition of Copernicus' *De revolutionibus*,[25] and Reinhold spread abroad the Copernican teaching by stating in the Preface to his widely-used *Prutenic Tables* that Copernicus was "an Atlas or a second Ptolemy" and that "we are greatly indebted" to him because "by publishing his work on the revolutions, he restored and recalled to light the teaching concerning the movements, which had almost collapsed."[26] The Copernican interests of the Wittenberg faculty are evident also from the fact that in 1542 one of Copernicus' writings was printed in Wittenberg by the very printer (Hans Lufft) who issued Luther's translation of the Bible.[27] As Elert has well said, "If the teaching of Copernicus was fostered at the universities at all, this took place in the domain of Lutheranism."[28]

---

[22] *WA — TR*, I 17.

[23] *WA — TR*, IV, 4705.

[24] *WA — TR*, II, 2730a.

[25] It is worthwhile noting that, some modern writers notwithstanding, when Rhaeticus later left Wittenberg for Leipzig, he did *not* do so because of persecution directed against his Copernicanism; this historical issue has been thoroughly aired by Elert (*op. cit.*, pp. 420-22) on the basis of the primary sources.

[26] Erasmus Reinhold, *Prutenicae Tabulae coelestium motuum* (Tübingen, 1551), Praefatio.

[27] Cf. Elert, *op. cit.*, p. 422.

[28] Ibid., p. 426.

But Lutheranism did not merely promulgate the Copernican system; it provided the ideological milieu for the refining, perfecting, and advancing of that view in the years that followed. Both Tycho Brahe, whose careful and systematic observations of stellar positions and development of powerful astronomical instruments were indispensable for later cosmological theorizing, and his assistant Johann Kepler, who went on to formulate the laws of planetary motion which have become fundamental to all of modern astronomy, were Lutherans. Kepler's *Prodromus* was edited by his former teacher, Michael Maestlin, a Lutheran pastor and "himself no mean astronomer."[29] The connecting link between Brahe and the Melanchthonian circle was the orthodox Lutheran theologian David Chytraeus, who was responsible (significantly) for the article on the Lord's Supper in the great Lutheran confessional document, the *Formula of Concord,* and whose *De sacrificiis* I have edited and translated for the first time.[30] Chytraeus, who had studied under both Luther and Melanchthon, dealt at some length with the new star of 1572 in his commentary on Deuteronomy, and published a separate treatise on the comet of 1577; as a result, Brahe and Chytraeus entered into correspondence.[31] Brahe's epochal works, *De nova stella* (on the star of 1572) and *De mundi aetherii recentioribus phaenomenis* (containing his account of the comet of 1577) demonstrate his concern with these phenomena; his observations of their lack of appreciable daily parallax led him to the revolutionary

---

[29] Thorndike, *op. cit.,* p. 412. Elert has shown (*op. cit.,* pp. 427-29) that although Kepler did run into theological difficulty because he could only subscribe to the Lutheran *Formula of Concord* "as one who confesses that here and there he is uncertain with respect to the construction and the pertinent words of a relation that is not clear," yet his basal Lutheranism is evident from the facts that he "had lost his position in Steiermark because of his profession of allegiance to the Augsburg Confession and, wherever he was, had always stayed with his church."

[30] John Warwick Montgomery (ed.), *Chytraeus on Sacrifice: A Reformation Treatise in Biblical Theology* (St. Louis, Mo.: Concordia Publishing House, 1962).

[31] See the Dreyer edition of Brahe's works, III, 225 ff. It is true that Brahe was not a Copernican, but, as Sarton has correctly noted, he had good reason, on the basis of his own highly accurate planetary observations, to question Copernicus: "Copernicus had been right to replace the sun in the center of our little universe, but he had continued to accept the old prejudice that every celestial trajectory is either circular, or a combination of circular motions. That fallacy was destroyed by the German Kepler in 1609; in the meanwhile, Brahe had been right to reject the Copernican system" (George Sarton, *The Appreciation of Ancient and Medieval Science during the Renaissance* [Philadelphia: University of Pennsylvania Press, 1955], p. 162).

conclusion that they belonged to the region of "fixed" stars, which according to the old Aristotelian world-view, remained physically unchangeable. Thus, in Jeans' words, Brahe "dealt a shattering blow to the Aristotelian cosmology."[32] Mention should also be made in passing of Johann Fabricius (d. 1587), who first observed sunspots and the rotation of the sun, and Samuel Dörffel (d. 1688), who first demonstrated the parabolic orbit of comets; Fabricius was a Lutheran layman, Dörffel a Lutheran pastor.[33]

What was the compelling motivation that brought about such extensive and important astronomical work among Lutheran scholars of the Reformation period? Some have argued that the impetus came from medieval astrology via the humanism of the Italian Renaissance, and that Melanchthon especially was an heir of this tradition. But, as Wedel has shown in his *Mediaeval Attitude toward Astrology,* the treatment of astrology by the great medieval theologians such as Aquinas was by no means unqualifiedly favorable, for (consistent with their theological synergism) they refused to place the human will under stellar influence, and they saw demonic influence at work in *per certitudinem* astrological prediction;[34] and the Italian Renaissance, though plagued with much superstitious popular astrology (Burckhardt describes it well in his *Civilization of the Renaissance in Italy*), heartily opposed astrological theory as detracting from anthropocentric freedom of the will. From Petrarch to Pico of Mirandola[35] we see the basic antagonism of Renaissance humanism to

[32] Sir James Jeans, *The Growth of Physical Science* (2d ed.; New York: Fawcett Premier Books, 1958), p. 128. The intimate connection between astronomy and astrology in Brahe's work is well illustrated by the fact that his study of the great comet of 1577 led him to predict that in the north, in Finland, a prince would be born who should lay waste Germany and vanish in 1632; Gustavus Adolphus was born in Finland, ravaged Germany during the Thirty Years' War, and was killed at Lützen in 1632! (Cf. Manly Hall, *The Story of Astrology* [Los Angeles: Phoenix Press, 1933], p. 29).

[33] Elert, *op. cit.,* p. 431.

[34] Theodore Otto Wedel, *The Mediaeval Attitude toward Astrology, particularly in England* ("Yale Studies in English," LX; New Haven: Yale University Press, 1920), pp. 67 ff. Contrast the mythological picture of Aquinas as a magician, as described by Gabriel Naudé in his *Apologie pour tous les grands personnages qui ont été faussement soupçonnés de Magie* (Paris, 1635), chaps. xvii-xviii.

[35] On Pico, cf. my article, "Eros and Agape in the Thought of Giovanni Pico della Mirandola," *Concordia Theological Monthly,* XXXII (December, 1961), 733-46. Pico's *Adversus astrologos,* written after his conversion, contains some excellent theological arguments against astrology, but strong emphasis is still placed upon an anthropocentric doctrine of the freedom of the will.

divine control of human affairs through the stars. Wedel regards
Petrarch's negative attitude both to astrology and to medicine
as manifesting his "indifference to science as a whole,"[36] and,
the unsystematic Leonardo da Vinci's scientific curiosity notwithstanding, this is not an inaccurate description of Renaissance humanism in general.[37]

The source of the Lutheran astrological-astronomical interests must be sought in the religious Reformation itself. This is
evident from the central theological concerns of the Lutheran
scholars who have just been discussed. Here we do not merely
refer to the theological supporters and promoters of the new
astronomy, such as Osiander, who arranged for the printing of
Copernicus' *De revolutionibus* and wrote a preface to it;[38] we
speak primarily of the Lutherans who actually engaged in astro-
nomical-astrological labors, such as Melanchthon, Brahe, and
Kepler. Melanchthon's preoccupation with astrology was based
not upon superstition, but upon the conviction that the regular-
ity of the heavenly phenomena displays the work of an "eternal
architectural Mind."[39] Here we have anything but a fatalistic,
deistic determinism; Melanchthon's theocentric belief that God
providentially guides the world through "secondary causes"[40]
is one with Luther's conviction that the risen Christ is dynamically present in even the apparently trivial natural occurrences
of the world. Melanchthon is really justifying astrology in terms
of the Pauline assertion (Rom. 8:28) that τοῖς ἀγαπῶσιν τὸν
θεὸν πάντα συνεργεῖ ὁ θεὸς εἰς ἀγαθόν ("in all things God works
for good with those who love Him"), and he thereby gives astrological and astronomical research a theological dynamic which
it heretofore lacked.

Tycho Brahe displays this same dynamic when he asserts
in his *De nova stella* that man should be "engaged constantly in

[36] Wedel, *op. cit.*, p. 86.

[37] Cf. Sarton's assertion (*op. cit.*, pp. 162-63): "In spite of Copernicus'
bold departure, the new astronomy is not his nor does it belong to the Renaissance; it was created by Kepler and Galileo in the seventeenth century.
As far as astronomy is concerned, the Renaissance was an age of disorder
and futile compromises."

[38] See Emanuel Hirsch, *Die Theologie des Andreas Osiander und ihre ge-
schichtlichen Voraussetzungen* (Göttingen: Vandenhoeck & Ruprecht, 1919),
pp. 118-22. Osiander's preface to the *De revolutionibus* is reprinted on p.
290 of Hirsch's work.

[39] *CR*, V, 819 ff.

[40] *CR*, XIII, 329. Cf. the remarks on this subject by the great Lutheran
dogmatician of the early Reformation period, Johann Gerhard, in his *Loci
theologici*, loc. 6, chaps. xii-xv (Preuss edition, II, 45-47).

the delightful consideration of the divine works that shine forth everywhere in the structure of the world."[41] As for Kepler, Ludwig Guenther has shown in his *Kepler und die Theologie* that this Lutheran father of modern astronomy was consistently and vitally concerned about theological issues;[42] his desire to ground his astronomical work in the Biblical revelation is evident from his detailed attempts to harmonize the cosmological passages of the Bible (especially the Joshua account of "the sun standing still") with the Copernican system.[43] It is as a spiritual heir of Luther that Kepler writes at the close of his *Harmony of the World*:[44]

> I thank Thee, O Lord, our Creator, that Thou hast permitted me to look at the beauty in Thy work of creation; I exult in the works of Thy hands. See, I have here completed the work to which I felt called; I have earned interest from the talent that Thou hast given me. I have proclaimed the glory of Thy works to the people who will read these demonstrations, to the extent that the limitations of my spirit would allow.

As Joseph Agassi of Hong Kong University points out in his exceedingly important *History and Theory* Beiheft, *Towards an Historiography of Science,* the theological sources of the scientific work of Brahe and Kepler have deeply troubled "inductivist" historians of science — those who still naively follow the Baconian assumption that scientific thought is purely a matter of induction based upon "open-minded" observation of facts.[45] In

[41] Tycho Brahe, *De nova stella,* ed. Regia Societas Scientiarum Danica (Hauniae [Copenhagen], 1901), fol. [E4]ᵛ. Elert (*op. cit.,* p. 442) is unfair to Tycho when he claims that Luther's "energizing factor is missing" in him; in actuality, it is this very evangelical energizing factor that motivates Tycho's astronomical labors!

[42] Ludwig Guenther, *Kepler und die Theologie* (Giessen: Alfred Töpelmann, 1905). Kepler's astrological concerns are set out in Norbert Herz's *Keplers Astrologie* (Wien, 1895).

[43] See especially Kepler's introduction to his *Astronomia nova* of 1609 (in the Frisch edition of Kepler's *Opera omnia,* III, 153. ff.).

[44] In Vol. V of the Frisch edition of Kepler's *Opera omnia.*

[45] Joseph Agassi, *Towards an Historiography of Science* ("History and Theory Beihefte," 2; The Hague: Mouton, 1963), pp. 13-14, 88-89, and *passim.* Cf. Herbert Butterfield's observation that the Copernican system was treated with more open-mindedness by astrologers than by others in the sixteenth century (*The Origins of Modern Science, 1300-1800* [London: G. Bell, 1957], p. 58).

actuality, the theocentric theology of such men as Brahe and Kepler profoundly influenced their scientific activity; to ignore or depreciate their beliefs is to cut ourselves off from the well-springs that fed their personalities and from the only adequate means of comprehending their work historically.

The intimate relation between theology and cosmological study in Lutheran circles during the Reformation period was given a theoretical basis in the almost forgotten work, *Astrology Theologized,* by the Lutheran pastor and mystic Valentin Weigel (1533-1588).[46] Weigel argues: "Every astrological gift, coming from the Light of Nature, ought to be ruled and subjected to the Divine Will by the Theological Spirit dwelling in us, that so the Will of the Lord be done, *as in heaven, so also in earth.* For all Wisdom, both Natural and Supernatural, is from the Lord."[47] Weigel places great stress on the providential action of God throughout His created universe — both in the stellar realm and in man himself. Here we have the union of the Macrocosm (the universe external to man) and the Microcosm (man himself, intimately reflecting God's external world) which, set out as a theme by Paracelsus,[48] and incorporated into the Lutheran dogmatics of the sixteenth century by such writers as Heerbrand,[49]

---

[46] Weigel's mysticism (which, admittedly, sometimes went to extremes) was severely condemned by some of his contemporary dogmaticians; this negativistic evaluation of Weigel is reflected in the brief article on him in the *Lutheran Cyclopedia,* ed. E. L. Lueker (St. Louis, Mo.: Concordia Publishing House, 1954), p. 1123. However, he has been properly rehabilitated by Alexandre Koyré in his *Mystiques, spirituels, alchemistes du XVIᵉ siècle allemand* (Paris: Armand Colin, 1955), pp. 81-116. It is noteworthy that Koyré parallels certain aspects of Weigel's thought with the Pauline mysticism that so profoundly affected Luther (cf. p. 115). The very fact that Weigel signed the Lutheran *Formula of Concord* says something as to his orthodoxy.

[47] Valentin Weigel, *"Astrology Theologized": The Spiritual Hermeneutics of Astrology and Holy Writ,* ed. Anna B. Kingsford (London: George Redway, 1866), p. 52. A. Israel has argued that this work was not written by Weigel, but Koyré (*op. cit.,* p. 82) rightly questions the general validity of Israel's critical judgments on Weigel. Thorndike totally misunderstands the purpose of the *Astrology Theologized* when he states that "observance of the Sabbath day seems the chief concern of the author" (*A History of Magic and Experimental Science,* VII [New York: Columbia University Press, 1958], 94).

[48] Cf. C. G. Jung, *Paracelsica: Zwei Vorlesungen ueber den Arzt und Philosophen Theophrastus* (Zürich: Rascher Verlag, 1942); and Henry M. Pachter, *Magic into Science: The Story of Paracelsus* (New York: Henry Schuman, 1951), especially chap. vii.

[49] Jakob Heerbrand, *Compendium theologiae* (Tubingae: G. Gruppenbach, 1579), pp. 37-38.

provides a unified, harmonized conception of the created universe. But with mention of Macrocosm and Microcosm we move into the second major area of Lutheran scientific activity during the Reformation era: the fascinating realm of alchemy.

CROSS AND CRUCIBLE

The popular conception of the alchemist as at best a simpleton or at worst a charlatan is, it would seem, a permanent heritage from the literary portraits drawn by Chaucer in his "Canon's Yeoman's Tale" and by Ben Jonson in his delightful play, *The Alchemist.*[50] Jonson's character Surly indelibly etches the stereotype when he asserts that

Alchemy is a pretty kind of game,
Somewhat like tricks o' the cards, to cheat a man
With charming.

The theoretical condemnations of alchemy by Francis Bacon and especially Robert Boyle (*The Sceptical Chymist*) were so devastating that it has not been until relatively recent times that the great significance of alchemy for the rise of modern chemistry has been recognized. Indeed, as late as 1949 Herbert Butterfield could write in his *Origins of Modern Science:* "The historians who specialize in this field seem sometimes to be under the wrath of God themselves; for, like those who write on the Bacon-Shakespeare controversy or on Spanish politics, they seem to become tinctured with the kind of lunacy they set out to describe."[51] But notwithstanding a few historians of science, such as A. R. Hall, who maintain that technological handbooks on smelting, assaying, etc., were more influential than alchemical experimentation for the rise of modern chemistry,[52] there is quite general agreement today that, in Read's words, we should despise neither the alchemists' "labourings nor their imaginings; for they followed, generation after generation, along a path that was destined to lead in a later age into the spacious domains of modern chemistry."[53] The very titles of recent works on the subject make this point very strongly; for example, F. Sherwood Taylor's

---

[50] Cf. John Read, *The Alchemist in Life, Literature and Art* (London: Thomas Nelson, 1947), pp. 27 ff.

[51] Butterfield, *op. cit.*, p. 129.

[52] A. R. Hall, *The Scientific Revolution, 1500-1800* (2d ed.; London: Longmans, 1962), pp. 69-70, 224, 308-309.

[53] Reda, *op. cit.*, p. 24.

The Alchemists, Founders of Modern Chemistry,[54] and Read's latest book, *Through Alchemy to Chemistry*.[55] L. W. H. Hull summarizes a part of the relevant evidence as follows:

> The alchemists discovered important substances, such as alcohol and the mineral acids, which turned out to have many uses in industry and in the gradual development of scientific chemistry. They also gained valuable knowledge of alloys and metallurgical processes. The development of optical glass was largely due to them. Much of the ordinary apparatus of chemistry, used for distillation, filtration and heating, was invented and improved by the alchemists.[56]

Now it is true that alchemy is not limited to the Western tradition (Caron and Hutin, among others, provide interesting insights into Chinese and Indian alchemy,[57] and Jung and Eliade see in alchemical operations manifestations of universal psychological and religious needs);[58] it is likewise true that in the West the origins of alchemy go back to earliest antiquity (as Berthelot and Hopkins have shown);[59] and it cannot be denied that a Christianization of alchemy occurred in the Middle Ages through the work of such hermetics as Arnold of Villanova.[60]

---

[54] F. Sherwood Taylor, *The Alchemists, Founders of Modern Chemistry* (London: William Heinemann, 1951).

[55] John Read, *Through Alchemy to Chemistry* (London: G. Bell, 1957).

[56] L. W. H. Hull, *History and Philosophy of Science* (London: Longmans, 1959), p. 119. Hull notes on p. 267 that the alchemists' use of astrological symbols for the metals served as a backdrop for modern chemical symbolism. See also the chapter titled, "Découvertes faites en chimie par les philosophes hermétiques," in the old but still important work by Louis Figuier, *L'Alchimie et les alchimistes* (3d ed.; Paris: Hachette, 1860), pp. 92-102.

[57] M. Caron and S. Hutin, *The Alchemists*, trans. Helen R. Lane ("Evergreen Profile Book," 27; New York: Grove Press, 1961), pp. 108-112. See also Taylor, *op. cit.*, pp. 68-75.

[58] Mircea Eliade, *The Forge and the Crucible*, trans. Stephen Corrin (New York: Harper, 1962), especially pp. 199-204 (on Jung). See also Eliade's "Note sur Jung et l'alchimie" in *Le Disque Vert: C. G. Jung* (Bruxelles, 1955), pp. 97-109.

[59] M. Berthelot, *Les origines de l'alchimie* (Paris: Steinheil, 1885); Arthur John Hopkins, *Alchemy, Child of Greek Philosophy* (New York: Columbia University Press, 1934). Hopkins' work is unfortunately marred by a naive eighteenth-century "Enlightenment" philosophy of history.

[60] On Arnold, see Albert Poisson (ed.), *Cinq traités d'alchimie* (Paris: Chacornac, 1890), pp. 5-21; and José Ramón de Luanco y Riego, *La alquimia en España* (2 vols.; Barcelona, 1889-1897), II, 103-141, 244-88.

Nonetheless, the greatest flowering of Christian alchemy co-
incided with the German Reformation of the sixteenth and seventeenth centuries.[61] Boyle testified to this fact when he once
spoke of German as the "Hermetical language," because so many
alchemists had used it.[62] A. E. White has demonstrated that
much of the alchemical labor of the time was carried on by Rosicrucian hermetics,[63] and though the Rosicrucian mysticism
eventually passed outside confessional Christianity, its roots
almost certainly lie in Lutheranism. Luther's heraldic seal displays a rose and a cross, and Roman Catholic critics of Rosicrucianism during the Reformation period pointed to its connection
with Lutheranism.[64]

What was Luther's attitude toward alchemy? Though he
did not agree with the extreme form of alchemical speculation
that wished to erase the God-established distinctions among
different species of reality,[65] his general attitude to alchemy could
hardly have been more favorable. Here is his fullest statement
on the subject, a statement employing standard alchemical terminology:

> The science of alchemy [ars alchimica] I like
> very well, and, indeed, it is truly the natural
> philosophy of the ancients. I like it not only for

---

[61] Jung writes: "Alchemy reached its greatest efflorescence in the sixteenth
and seventeenth centuries, then to all appearances it began to die out. In
reality it found its continuation in natural science" (Aion: Researches into
the Phenomenology of the Self, trans. R. F. C. Hull ["Collected Works,"
IX/2; New York: Bollingen Foundation, 1959], p. 176). In spite of oft-repeated statements to the contrary, alchemy "played only a very subordinate
part at the best period of the Renaissance" (Jacob Burckhardt, The Civilization of the Renaissance in Italy, trans. S. G. C. Middlemore [3d. ed.; London: Phaidon Press, 1950], p. 334). Leonardo da Vinci makes scornful references to alchemy (and astrology) in his Notebooks.

[62] Hall, op. cit., p. 224. Cf. also Charles Mackay, Extra-ordinary Popular
Delusions (reprint ed.; [New York?]: L. C. Page, 1932), pp. 152 ff.

[63] See Waite's classic, The Brotherhood of the Rosy Cross (reprint ed.;
New Hyde Park, New York: University Books, 1961).

[64] E.g., Jacques Gaulthier (Gualterius), S. J. (1560-1636), suggests in his
Table chronographique de l'estat du Christianisme (Lyon, 1633), pp. 889 ff.,
that "ceste prétendue Fraternité n'est ni si ancienne qu'elle se fait, ains que
c'est un rejetton du Luthérianisme, meslangé par Satan d'empirisme et de
magie, pour mieux decevoir les esprits volages et curieux." Mackay (op.
cit., pp. 194-95) is in actuality referring to this passage when he writes: "The
Abbé Gaultier, a Jesuit, wrote a book [sic] to prove that, by their enmity
to the pope, they [the Rosicrucians] could be no other than disciples of
Luther sent to promulgate his heresy."

[65] WA — TR, V. 5671.

the many uses it has in decocting metals and
in distilling and sublimating herbs and liquors
[*in excoquendis metallis, item herbis et liquori-
bus distillandis ac sublimandis*], but also for the
sake of the allegory and secret signification,
which is exceedingly fine, touching the resurrection of the dead at the Last Day. For, as in
a furnace the fire extracts and separates from a
substance the other portions, and carries up-
ward the spirit, the life, the sap, the strength,
while the unclean matter, the dregs, remain at
the bottom, like a dead and worthless carcass
[here Luther illustrates further with the preparation of wine, cinnamon, and nutmeg], even so
God, at the day of judgment, will separate all
things through fire, the righteous from the un-
godly.[66]

Luther in his characteristic fashion praises alchemy both for its
practical usefulness *per se* and for its ability to witness to basic
Christian truth; as we shall see, these dual emphases run through
all of the Lutheran alchemy of the period. The Reformer's
positive attitude toward the hermetic art is also attested, though
indirectly, by the vocation of his son Paul. Paul Luther, we
learn from the primary-source funeral oration delivered for him
by Matthias Dresser in 1593, was a court physician who employed *aurum potabile* ("potable gold") in his practice.[67] Thus
Martin Luther's son was certainly well acquainted with the iatro-
chemical tradition so greatly influenced by Paracelsus.

Limitations of space prevent us from meeting more than a
few of the many Lutheran alchemists of the Reformation era.
We shall concentrate on four great hermetics who can respectively
illustrate for us the chemical, the allegorical, the theological, and
the existential aspects of Lutheran alchemy.

Andreas Libavius, M.D. (1550-1616) was concerned primarily with the chemical and medical ramifications of alchemy; his

---

[66] *WA — TR*, I, 1149.

[67] Printed by Melchior Adam in his *Vitae Germanorum medicorum* (Hai-
delbergae: J. Rosa, 1620), pp. 338-42 (the "medicamenta a Luthero in of-
ficinis" are listed on p. 340). With the iatrochemists' medicinal use of gold,
cf. present-day chrysotherapy (see, e.g., Eugene F. Traut, *Rheumatic Dis-
eases, Diagnosis and Treatment* [St. Louis, Mo.: Mosby, 1952], chap.
xlvii ["Gold and Other Heavy Metals in Arthritis"], pp. 850-55).

works demonstrate beyond question the significant contribution of Reformation alchemy to the rise of modern chemistry. Read thus describes his classic work, the *Alchymia:*

> This truly massive work, of which the 1606 edition weighs about ten pounds, is a blend of alchemical mysticism and symbolism with sound chemical knowledge. Besides the emblematic designs, it contains clear drawings of apparatus, and even of a "chemical house," or laboratory shown both in plan and elevation. This formidable work has sometimes been termed the first text-book of chemistry, since it contains clear descriptions of so many chemical substances and processes, including "spiritus fumans Libavii" (stannic chloride), sugar of lead, sulphate of ammonia, the burning of sulphur with saltpetre to give oil of vitriol, the preparation of sugar candy, and the extraction of alcohol from fermented liquors.[68]

That his Lutheran theology was the motivating power behind Libavius' alchemical activities is shown by his defense of the thesis that "it is absurd not to posit God as present in everything,"[69] and by his support of the Aristotelian-Melanchthonian multiple-method approach to knowledge over against the "single-method deduction" of the Calvinist Ramus. Libavius "regarded as unattainable their [the Ramists'] ideal of limiting each art to deduction from a set of homogeneous, self-evident and germane axioms, since he held that God alone knew all the details of art and nature well enough to lay down as a starting-point such impeccable axioms and scientific rules for constituting arts."[70] This defense of the Melanchthonian approach, incidentally, points up the basic fallacy in Gilbert's recent argument that the Melanchthonian methodology contributed little to the rise of seventeenth-

---

[68] Read, *Through Alchemy to Chemistry,* pp. 92-93. Excellent drawings of chemical apparatus are also provided in the first part of Libavius' *Praxis alchymiae* (Frankfurt: Kopff, 1604).

[69] Libavius, *Tractatus duo physici* (Frankfurt, 1594); see Thorndike, *A History of Magic and Experimental Science,* VI (New York: Columbia University Press, 1941), 239.

[70] Ibid., p. 238.

century science;[71] in actuality, it was the very breadth of the Melanchthonian approach that made it so hospitable to experimental induction such as the Lutheran alchemists employed.[72] And as we see from Libavius' defense of this approach, its breadth was an inevitable corollary of Lutheran theocentrism.

The allegorical flavor of Reformation alchemy is well illustrated by Heinrich Khunrath (1560-1605), a physician and mystic who, to use Waite's expression, regarded "the whole cosmos as a work of Supernal Alchemy, performed in the crucible of God."[73] For Khunrath the alchemical quest of the Philosopher's Stone was a quest to reveal the true wholeness of the physical universe (the Macrocosm) on the basis of Christ's restoration of wholeness to man (the Microcosm). Because of the harmonic relation subsisting between man and the universe, between Microcosm and Macrocosm, Khunrath conceives of the Stone as the *Filius Macrocosmi* ("the Son of Macrocosm") and identifies it with Christ Himself.[74] When Khunrath speaks of the color of the Stone as "rosy-colored blood," he is allegorically expressing his belief that the Christ of the Cross is not only the sole source of man's salvation but also the sole answer to man's quest to find meaning in the external world; conversely, he is saying that the investigation of the physical universe is actually a quest for Christ, since Christ is really present in it. Two of the allegorical illustrations in Khunrath's *Amphitheatrum sapi-*

---

[71] Neal W. Gilbert, *Renaissance Concepts of Method* (New York: Columbia University Press, 1960), especially pp. 108-115, 125-28, 221-31. An examination of my personal copy of one of the greatest Lutheran methodological treatises of the Reformation period (Nicolaus Hemming[sen]'s *De methodis libri duo* [Lipsiae: J. Steinman, 1578]), which Gilbert did not consult but cites on the basis of secondary sources (pp. 112, 197), revealed the true breadth of the Melanchthonian approach (Hemming[sen] had studied under Melanchthon) and the degree to which Gilbert caricatures it. It is of interest that Tycho Brahe convinced Hemming[sen] that Calvin's arguments against astrology lacked theological validity (Thorndike, *op. cit.,* VI, 523).

[72] Indeed, Libavius would have less time spent on the abstract discussion of Peripatetic vs. Ramist method; he prefers actual scientific investigation to methodological dissensions and hatreds, which handicap scientific progress (see Libavius' *Quaest. physicarum controversarum inter Peripateticos et Rameos* of 1591).

[73] A. E. Waite, *The Sceret Tradition in Alchemy* (London: Kegan Paul, 1926), p. 254.

[74] Khunrath writes: "Since God the Lord for our edification permits Jesus Christ to be represented in the great Book of Nature by the Stone of the Philosophers, I may fitly quote the words of Isaiah the Prophet concerning Christ, in order thereby to show to some extent the wonderful harmony and

entiae aeternae [75] well attest to the theocentricity of his alchemical philosophy. One depicts "the alchemic citadel," surrounded by twenty-one supposed entrances — twenty of which are blind alleys, with the true path requiring faith and uprightness of heart; the second allegory displays the alchemist's chamber, where both experiments and prayer are carried on:

THE LUTHERAN ALCHEMIST'S "LAB-ORATORIUM"

By an ingenious play upon words he calls it "Lab-Oratorium," intending to express in this way, as other alchemists have already taught us, that the Stone is a blessing to be obtained only

correspondence of these two stones" (*Vom hylealischen . . . Chaos* [reprint ed.; Frankfurt, 1707], p. 17). There is, of course, explicit use of the imagery of Christ as a Rock or Stone in the Bible (e.g., Eph. 2:20; I Pet. 2:4-8). A. E. Waite (*The Secret Tradition in Alchemy*, p. 346 and *passim*) maintains that Khunrath was the first alchemist specifically to identify the Stone with Christ; although Jung has shown that such identification had previously occurred in the medieval period (*Psychology and Alchemy*, trans. R. F. C. Hull ["Collected Works," XII; New York: Bollingen Foundation, 1953], pp. 343, 360, 379), Khunrath's emphatic Biblical Christocentricity is exceedingly striking and would be inexplicable apart from the theological concerns of the Reformation.

[75] Thorndike is excessively critical of this work (*op. cit.*, VII, 273-75). A sympathetic treatment of Khunrath is given by Waite in his *Brotherhood of the Rosy Cross*, pp. 61 ff.

from God Himself, and that the efforts of the
adept will only be crowned with success if he
prays the Creator of all things to lend His aid
to a work which is a minute imitation of the
Creation. This is why Khunrath has shown himself on the left, praying to God before a tent,
in imitation of the Israelites in the desert. The
incense smokes, and Solomon's Seal shines upon
the table. To the right of this sumptuous gal-
lery, which to-day would be the Hall of State
of some *Rathaus* in an old German town, the
laboratory is seen, fitted with alchemic apparatus.[76]

The general influence of Khunrath's views in Lutheran circles is
fully demonstrated by the single fact that the great Lutheran
Pietist and devotional writer Johann Arndt (author of *True
Christianity*) wrote a commentary on the *Amphitheatrum*.[77]

The specific significance of Lutheran doctrine for Reformation alchemy can be seen in the work of Michael Maier (1568-
1622), Count Palatine, doctor of medicine and of philosophy,
who, along with Brahe and Kepler, served at the court of Holy
Roman Emperor Rudolph II. Maier produced numerous alchemical works, and wrote in support of an evangelical Rosicrucianism.[78] In his largest work, the *Symbola aureae mensae,*

---

[76] Grillot de Givry, *Witchcraft, Magic & Alchemy,* trans. J. Courtenay
Locke ([New York?]: Frederick Publications, 1954), p. 383. The two illustrations from the *Amphitheatrum* are reproduced on pp. 348, 384.

[77] Arndt's tract is titled, *Judicium über die vier Figuren des grossen Am-
phitheatri Henrici Khunraths,* and was printed in: (1) Khunrath's *De igne
magorum philosophorumque secreto externo et visibili* (Strassburg, 1608);
(2) Khunrath's *Trinum chymicum secundum* (Strassburg, 1700) [another
edition of the *De igne*]; and (3) the *Chymisches Lust-Gärtlein* (Ludwigs-
burg: C. H. Pfotenhauer, 1747), pp. 87-96. The citations of (1) and (2) are
given in the *Catalogue of the Ferguson Collection . . . in the Library of the
University of Glasgow* (2 vols.; Glasgow: Robert Maclehose, 1943), I, 367;
item (3) is listed in John Ferguson's *Bibliotheca Chemica* (2 vols.; Glasgow: James Maclehose, 1906), I, 48, 159, 463.

[78] An excellent chapter devoted to Maier appears in Waite's *Brotherhood
of the Rosy Cross,* pp. 310-39. Maier is frequently cited by Jung in his
Psychology and Alchemy, but, in line with Jung's syncretic presuppositions,
he is discussed indiscriminately with non-Christian alchemists. Unfortunately
it must be said that Jung (like Eliade from the standpoint of general his-
tory-of-religions) misses the unique character of Christian alchemy by in-
sisting that "Christ" is in the final analysis but an ideogram of the self
(Jung, *Aion,* pp. 36-71, 173-83; *Answer to Job,* trans. R. F. C. Hull [Lon-
don: Routledge & Kegan Paul, 1954], *passim*).

Maier affirms the indissoluble connection between the cardinal Lutheran doctrine of the Real Presence and the alchemical aim of transforming the external world through the discovery of the "Philosopher's Stone," i.e., through the discovery of Christ's presence in both macrocosmic and microcosmic reality. A woodcut depicts the Alchemist in full eucharistic vestments saying mass at an altar, and the corresponding text indicates that

> He [Maier] saw the perfection of it [the hermetic "work"] in the birth of the Philosophic Stone in the Sacred Nativity; its sublimation in the life and passion; dark and black in the death; then in the resurrection and life, the red and perfect colour. This comparison he found in the nativity, life, passion, death, and resurrection of Christ as commemorated in the Eucharist. Thus earthly things are the pictures of the heavenly, "Lapis itaque ut Homo" [Man therefore becomes like the Stone, i.e., like Christ].[79]

The explicit connection between earth and heaven is indicated by Maier in his *De circulo physico, quadrato* when he affirms his belief that "this whole world is an open book teaching rational men in general the existence and nature of God, the transitory character of this life, and the need to look to another life for eternal felicity."[80]

The obvious movement in the direction of an existential Christ-mysticism in Maier is even more pronounced in the dazzlingly beautiful *Chymical Wedding* of "Christian Rosencreutz," a pseudonym of Johann Valentin Andreae (1586-1654), who is best known for his "decidedly Lutheran"[81] utopian work, *Christianopolis*. Though vocationally a pastor, Andreae had a strong interest in science, as is evidenced by his study of mathematics under Maestlin (whom we have already met as Kepler's

---

[79] J. B. Craven, *Count Michael* Maier, *Life and Writings* (Kirkwall [Eng.]: William Peace, 1910), pp. 82-83. Maier's *Subtle Allegory concerning the Secrets of Alchemy* is available in English translation in *The Hermetic Museum, Restored and Enlarged,* ed. A. E. Waite (2 vols.; London: James Elliott, 1893), II, 199-223.

[50] Michael Maier, *De circulo physico, quadrato: hoc est. Auro, eiusque virtute medicinali* (Oppenheimii, 1616), chap. vii, pp. 43-49.

[81] The words are Troeltsch's (*The Social Teaching of the Christian Churches* [*op. cit.* in note 8], II, 570). Troeltsch calls Andreae "one of the finest and most original Lutheran thinkers."

teacher) and by the correspondence which he maintained with Kepler until the latter's death.[82] Widely — and incorrectly — regarded as author of the *Fame* and *Confession of the Fraternity of R ∴ C ∴* ,[83] the earliest explicitly Rosicrucian documents, Andreae had a profound (albeit unwitting) effect on the subsequent history of Rosicrucianism.[84] Andreae's *Chymical Wedding* is a lavish tapestry of alchemical and theological symbolism, and we can do no more here than to point up several of its most suggestive pictorial devices. First, the Cross of Christ is the starting-point for the entire alchemical drama; "Rosencreutz" (Andreae) receives his invitation to the Royal Wedding (symbolizing the production of the Philosopher's Stone through the traditional "marriage" of the opposite principles "Sulphur" and "Mercury") on the eve before Easter when he is preparing unleavened bread in his heart and in the presence of the Paschal Lamb; the invitation is sealed with a cross and the words, "In hoc signo vinces."[85] Secondly, an existential union with God on the microcosmic level is suggested by Rosencreutz's reception of wounds in his feet, or stigmata.[86] Thirdly, a macrocosmic fulfilment is symbolized by a room with a golden globe in the center on which the sun's light is concentrated from all sides; thus, in philosophical terms, the Many become One for Rosencreutz as the seemingly contrary and inexplicable elements in the universe

---

[82] See Felix Emil Held (ed.), *Johann Valentin Andreae's Christianopolis: An Ideal State of the Seventeeth Century* ([Urbana, Ill.]: University of Illinois, 1914), p. 12.

[83] Published pseudonymously in English translation (London, 1652) by "Eugenius Philalethes" (Thomas Vaughan). See A. E. Waite (ed.), *The Works of Thomas Vaughan* (London: Theosophical Publishing House, 1919), pp. 339-82 and 490. Cf. also R. Kienast, *Johann Valentin Andreae und die vier echten Rosenkreutzer-Schriften* ("Palaestra," 152; Leipzig: Mayer & Müller, 1926).

[84] See section III.C. ("Andreae and the Occult Tradition") of my doctoral dissertation, "Cross and Crucible: Johann Valentin Andreae's *Chymical Wedding* in the Original German Text (1616) and in the Historic Foxcroft English Translation (1690), with Biographical-Theological Introduction, Notes, and Bibliography" (Université de Strasbourg, Faculté de Théologie Protestante, 1964). A slightly revised version of this work is scheduled for immediate publication in two volumes in the monographic series, "International Archives of the History of Ideas" (The Hague: Martinus Nijhoff).

[85] Cf. Waite, *The Brotherhood of the Rosy Cross*, pp. 160 ff. For Jung's views on Andreae, see his *Practice of Psychotherapy*, trans. R. F. C. Hull ("Collected Works," XVI; New York: Bollingen Foundation, 1954), pp. 209, 216, 286, 289 (and cf. my note 78 above).

[86] Johann Valentin Andreae, *The Hermetick Romance or the Chymical Wedding*, trans. E. Foxcroft (London, 1690), p. 17.

conjoin.[87] Significantly, this is the key point in the entire nar-
rative, for here "rebirth begins to replace death."[88] In spite of
the later use of Andreae's *Chymical Wedding* by those preferring
general religious mysticism to Reformation theology (Goethe was
influenced by Andreae's work, and in the great poet we see a
pantheizing of the alchemical tradition[89]), yet Andreae beauti-
fully expresses the longing of the Lutheran hermetics to conjoin
Macrocosm and Microcosm through the recognition of Christ's
centrality in both, and thereby to infuse all of created reality
with the truth of the Gospel. A by-product of this dream, as we
have already noted, was an intense desire to investigate the
chemical nature of the physical world and apply the results of
such investigation to the healing of human ills.

CROSS AND CONTEMPORANEITY

If we agree that Lutheranism significantly influenced the
progress of science through astrological-astronomical and alchem-
ical-chemical activity during the Reformation period, we must
ask one further question: Do the speculations of the long-for-
gotten thinkers here discussed have anything relevant to say
to contemporary philosophy of science? On the surface, the
answer might seem to be a simple No, since it would be absurd
to suggest a revival of astrology and alchemy *per se*. However,
I believe that through its unifying root principle Reformation
Lutheran astrology and alchemy can say something exceedingly important in the present scientific milieu.

The science of the mid-twentieth century is faced by three
over-arching problems: (1) runaway specialization and fragmentation that make workers even in the same scientific discipline increasingly unable to communicate with each other,
(2) the creation of what C. P. Snow has called "the two cultures," that is to say, the separation of the sciences from the
humanities and the humanities from the sciences,[90] and (3) the

---

[87] Ibid., pp. 150-51. On the important alchemical concept of the "conjunction of opposites," see Jung's *Mysterium Coniunctionis,* trans. R. F. C. Hull
("Collected Works," XIV; New York: Bollingen Foundation, 1963). With
the "conjunction" cf. Luther's concept of the "hidden" and "revealed" God
(*Deus absconditus et revelatus*).

[88] Ronald D. Gray, *Goethe the Alchemist* (Cambridge: Cambridge University Press, 1952), p. 207.

[89] Gray (*ibid.*) shows how Goethe pantheized the Lutheran alchemy of
Andreae and of the historian-pietist Gottfrid Arnold.

[90] C. P. Snow, *The Two Cultures and the Scientific Revolution* (New York:
Cambridge University Press, 1959); *Recent Thoughts on the Two Cultures*
(London, 1961).

disappearance of a sense of ultimate purpose or significance in scientific research (this disenchantment is well described by Werner Heisenberg in his essay "The Representation of Nature in Contemporary Physics,"[91] and by Daniel Bell in his little book, *Work and Its Discontents*[92]), and with this loss of meaning, a tendency to absolve science of the necessity of making moral decisions of any kind.

The Reformation thinkers treated in this paper would have been utterly amazed at these problems — all three of them. "Why," they would say to us, "how can you allow nature to be compartmentalized, or man to be separated from nature, or nature to be disengaged from its ultimate, Divine source, when the Real Presence of God infuses everything that is?" To the Lutheran astrologer or alchemist of the Reformation, nature was basically unified because the living God dynamically imparts His life to it (the alchemists even employed organic analogy to describe inorganic metallic change[93]), man and nature were essentially one, for man is a little world (a Microcosm) corresponding to and reflecting the characteristics of the universe about him (the Macrocosm); and ultimate purpose and meaning are the very substance of the universe, since the Christ who died to restore man is, again to use Luther's words, "even in the most insignificant leaf of a tree."

We have, of course, begun to see that every scientist must strive to become a generalist as well as a specialist, and both virology and psychosomatic medicine are properly breaking down an absolute distinction between Microcosm and Macrocosm;[94] but we still have a long way to go, particularly in find-

---

[91] In English translation in: Rollo May (ed.), *Symbolism in Religion and Literature* (New York: George Braziller, 1960), pp. 215-32.

[92] Boston: Beacon Press, 1956. Cf. also Eliade's *The Forge and the Crucible* (*op. cit.* in note 58 above).

[93] This organic view of the alchemists is very effectively explained in a manner understandable to the modern mind in Stephen Toulmin's *Foresight and Understanding: An Enquiry into the Aims of Science* ([Bloomington, Ind.]: Indiana University Press, 1961), pp. 69-81. Luther's thought was profoundly "organic" in character, as Joseph Sittler has shown in his *Structure of Christian Ethics* (Baton Rouge, La.: Louisiana State University Press, 1958).

[94] The desperate personal desire of some in our time to induce the blending of Macrocosm with Microcosm by artificial means is evidenced by Zen-Buddhist Alan Watts' experiments with lysergic acid diethylamide (LSD); see his chapter titled (significantly) "The New Alchemy," in his *This is IT and Other Essays on Zen and Spiritual Experience* (New York: Pantheon Books, 1960), pp. 125-53. Cf. also my article, "The Gospel according to LSD," *Christianity Today*, X (July 8, 1966), 44.

ing purpose and ethical significance for our scientific labors in a thermonuclear age. Torrance has recently argued that Calvinism gave great impetus to scientific development by regarding the "creation as something utterly distinct" from the Creator; thus "the element of real contingency" was introduced into Western thinking and the investigation of the physical world could begin in earnest.[95] I shall not dispute this contention, but I seriously wonder if our modern world has not succeeded so well in distinguishing itself from its Creator that for all practical purposes He no longer exists at all in the scientific realm? John Baillie has well written in his *Natural Science and the Spiritual Life*:

> When nature is believed to have no preordained meaning or purpose in itself, the speculative interest in it fails, and the remaining concern is only to subdue its inherent purposelessness to our own chosen ends. Yet if, in their turn, these ends of ours are not themselves informed by faith, if they are merely chosen and not prescribed, if they represent only human preferences dictated by interest instead of solemn obligations emanating from a source beyond ourselves, then science becomes a desperately dangerous tool to put in men's hands.[96]

Perhaps the time has now come, when, both out of sheer necessity and out of deep longing, we must return to the conception of a laboratory as simultaneously *laboratorium* and *oratorium*, in which we pray with Kepler: "I thank Thee, O Lord, our Creator, that Thou hast permitted me to look at the beauty in Thy work of creation; I exult in the works of Thy hands."

---

[95] Torrance, *Dialog*, II (Winter, 1963), 41 (cited above in note 9).

[96] John Baillie, *Natural Science and the Spiritual Life* (London: Oxford University Press, 1951), pp. 35-36.

SCHOLAR'S STUDY IN LUTHER'S DAY

III

LUTHER, LIBRARIES, AND LEARNING

Reformation history and sixteenth-century bibliographical history are inextricably related. Reformation scholar Harold J. Grimm writes: "The importance of printing in the spread of the Reformation can scarcely be exaggerated; but the Reformation also furthered the development of printing";[1] and Alfred Hessel, the library historian, states: "The Reformation forms an epoch in the history of libraries."[2] But generalizations are dangerous, and even the best generalizations gain in significance when illuminated by specific studies of the facts and interpretations supporting them. In the following pages an attempt will be made to shed further light on the interrelation of religious history and library history through an analysis of the attitude of the chief sixteenth-century reformer toward books and libraries. The techniques of the newer Luther research, stemming largely from the work of Karl Holl in Germany, will be utilized to answer the questions: What was Luther's position toward and contribution to the diffusion of knowledge through library development? What led the reformer to his characteristic bibliological phillosophy?

A PERSISTENT ALLEGATION

When Luther's Ninety-five Theses were forwarded to Rome and were read by Pope Leo X, a tradition credits the Pope with saying: "These have been written by a drunken German. He will feel different when he is sober."[3] This statement is of doubtful authenticity, but it well reveals an initial reaction on the part of Luther's theological opponents: Luther need not be taken seriously from an intellectual standpoint. It was not long, however, before negative criticism took a far more definite position, namely, that Luther and the movement he represented were in the most pronounced way deleterious to the progress of learning. Ten years after the posting of the Theses, Erasmus — the prince of humanists, who, as a contemporary aphorism put it, "laid the

---

[1] *The Reformation Era* (New York: Macmillan Co., 1954), p. 160. Cf. Pierce Butler, *An Introduction to Library Science* ("Phoenix Book" [Chicago: University of Chicago Press, 1961], p. 96: "The Protestant Reformation was in part actuated by the shift in public ideas and opinion, produced in six decades by the invention of printing." The vital role of the press in the early years of the Reformation is emphasized by Maurice Gravier, *Luther et l'opinion publique* (Paris: Aubier, [1942]).

[2] *A History of Libraries,* trans. Reuben Peiss (Washington, D.C.: Scarecrow Press, 1950), p. 51.

[3] *Tischreden* (hereinafter cited as *TR*), 2635 *a* and *b*, in the standard, critical *Weimarer Ausgabe* (hereinafter cited as *WA*) of Luther's works. Luther commented: "Ita alii omnes me a principio alto supercilio contemnebant."

egg that Luther hatched" — wrote to the great Nuremberg biblio-
phile Willibald Pirkheimer: "Wherever Lutheranism prevails,
there we see the downfall of learning."[4] Erasmus' judgment has
been repeatedly expressed down to our own time. It is not from a
Roman Catholic apologist, but from the great educational historian Friedrich Paulsen, that the following statement comes:
"Nor did he [Luther] cherish any strong desire for learning and
education; these things were far removed from his main interest,
and those who pursued them as the most vital aims of life, like
Erasmus of Rotterdam, he looked upon without sympathy, if
not with suspicion."[5]

On what grounds is Luther viewed as an opponent of
learning and culture, and by that fact, of books and libraries, the
tools of learning? Four principal arguments are most commonly
adduced, and they deserve examination here.

First was Luther's act of book burning. When the bull of excommunication (*Exsurge Domine*) reached Luther, he proceeded, on December 10, 1520, to burn it, together with books of
canon law and scholastic theology. This occurred at a mass meeting of Wittenberg University faculty and students — a meeting
to which Luther had invited the participants by public notice.
The books burned included Gratian's *Decretum,* the *Decretals,*
the *Clementines* and the *Extravagants,* Angelo Carletti di Chi-
vasso's *Summa Angelica* (a standard work on the sacrament of
penance at that time), books by Luther's theological nemesis
Johann Eck, and some volumes by Jerome Emser, also a bitter
controversialist against Luther.[6]

Second was Luther's anti-humanist and anti-liberal expressions of opinion. In his dispute with Erasmus on the freedom of

---

[4] "Ubicunque regnat Luteranismus, ibi litterarum est interitus; et tamen
hoc genus hominum maxime litteris alitur. Duo tantum querunt, censum
et uxorem; cetera praestat illis Evangelium, hoc est potestatem vivendi ut
velint" (letter of March 20, 1528; Erasmus, *Opus epistolarum,* ed. P. S. Allen
et al. [12 vols. Oxford: Clarendon Press, 1906-58], VII, 366).

[5] Friedrich Paulsen, *German Education Past and Present,* trans. T. Lorenz
(London: T. Fisher Unwin, 1908), p. 48. The same general interpretation
is presented in Paulsen's monumental *Geschichte des gelehrten Unterrichts,*
Vol. I (3d ed.; Leipzig: Veit, 1919).

[6] Four folios and about twelve smaller volumes were burned in all. See
WA, VII, 161-85; *BR* (Luther's *Briefwechsel,* in *WA*), 361; cf. M. Perlbach
and J. Luther, "Ein neuer Bericht über Luthers Verbrennung der Bann-
bulle," *Sitzungsberichte der königlich preussischen Akademie der Wissen-
schaften,* 1907, pp. 95-102; and G. Kawerau, "Fünfundzwanzig Jahre Luther-
forschung," *Theologische Studien und Kritiken,* LXXXI (1908), 587-88.

the will, Luther took a most rigorous predestinarian position. Such a position, it is argued, destroys human liberty and man's dignity,[7] and inevitably produces a narrow, illiberal attitude with regard to culture and learning. Thus it is by no means strange to find in Luther's writings such statements as the following, which in 1539 he prefaced to an early collected edition of his German works:

> I would gladly have seen all my books forgotten and destroyed. And among my reasons is my fear of the example. For I clearly see what benefit the fact has brought to the Church that men have begun to collect many books and great libraries outside and alongside Holy Scripture and have especially begun to pick up, without any distinction in particular, all sorts of fathers, councils, and doctors. . . . Although it is useful and necessary that the writings of some of the fathers and councils should be kept as witnesses and histories, nevertheless, I think, *Est modus in rebus,* and no harm has been done by the fact that the books of many of the fathers and councils have, by God's grace, been lost. For had all of them remained, one would scarcely be able to go in or out for books, and yet they would have presented nothing better than we find in Holy Scripture.[8]

A third point is the decline of educational institutions in the German lands during the early years of the Reformation. In an article which appeared on the quadricentennial of the posting of the Ninety-five Theses, the educational historian, Harry G. Good, stated: "In the parts of Germany where the Reformation was accepted much confusion was caused by the transfer from the Catholic to the Protestant beliefs, modes of worship and methods of church government; and in consequence education ceased to flourish."[9] Good supports this assertion with the

---

[7] So, in effect, argues Margaret Mann Phillips, *Erasmus and the Northern Renaissance* (London: English Universities Press, 1949), chap. v ("The Lutheran Tragedy"), pp. 150-201.

[8] *WA,* L, 657 ff.

[9] Harry G. Good, "The Position of Luther upon Education," *School and Society,* VI (November 3, 1917), 513.

following evidence in his standard work, *A History of Western Education:*

> School and university attendance declined rapidly in the period. The universities of Erfurt and Rostock never recovered from the losses sustained; but the numbers at Cologne, Vienna, Leipzig, and Basel also were greatly reduced. Professorships were abandoned because there were no students to be taught. Only little Wittenberg, founded in 1502, said Luther, is doing its best; but even Wittenberg lost three-fourths of its enrollment in the disastrous 1520's.[10]

Finally, the destruction of libraries was a result and by-product of reforming zeal. "Not infrequently, at the dissolution of German monasteries and religious institutions, the acquisitions resulting from many centuries of zealous collecting were carelessly disposed of or destroyed as papist literature."[11] Vorstius informs us that in the 1525 uprising of Thuringian peasants — an uprising motivated at least in part by "left-wing" Reformation ideas — a total of seventy monastic cloisters were plundered.[12] In many respects the bibliothecal situation in England during the sixteenth century was even more unfortunate,[13] and since Lutheran influence on the English reformation was very considerable,[14] some of the responsibility for English book losses is likewise laid at Luther's door.

[10] Harry G. Good, *A History of Western Education* (New York: Macmillan Co., 1947), p. 156. This argument (which comprises only one aspect of Good's over-all presentation of the educational effects of the Reformation) is set forth in great detail by the well-known Roman Catholic apologist-historian Hartmann Grisar in *Luther,* trans. E. M. Lamond; ed. Luigi Cappadelta, VI (London: Kegan Paul, 1917), 3-41.

[11] Hessel, *loc. cit.*

[12] Joris Vorstius, *Grundzüge der Bibliotheksgeschichte* (5th ed.; Leipzig: Harrassowitz, 1954), p. 31. Such losses are discussed in detail by Karl Schottenloher, "Schicksale von Büchern und Bibliotheken im Bauernkrieg," *Zeitschrift für Bücherfreunde,* XII, No. 2 (1908/1909), 396-408. Cf. *Handbuch der Bibliothekswissenschaft,* ed. Fritz Milkau and Georg Leyh, III, Pt. 1 (2d ed.; Wiesbaden: Harrassowitz, 1955), 562-63.

[13] See C. E. Wright, "The Dispersal of the Libraries in the Sixteenth Century," in *The English Library before 1700,* ed. Francis Wormald and C. E. Wright (London: University of London, Athlone Press, 1958), pp. 148-75.

[14] Cf. Henry Eyster Jacobs, *The Lutheran Movement in England during the Reigns of Henry VIII and Edward VI* (Philadelphia: G. W. Frederick, 1890).

THE EVIDENCE EXAMINED

How valid are the foregoing arguments as demonstrations of an anti-intellectual, anti-bibliothecal spirit in Luther and his movement? Such evidence cannot simply be discounted; the very persistency with which these negative criticisms are reiterated suggests that they contain some element of truth. Although it was not by choice, Luther did become the leader of one of the most powerful revolutions that Western civilization has undergone, and it is of the nature of revolutions to tear down in order to rebuild. Luther was convinced (and modern study has borne him out) that the scholastic educational system of the medieval church was one of its central pillars; Luther and his followers demanded thoroughgoing educational reform, and this reform sometimes entailed strong measures. But the real issue is not whether some tearing down preceded Reformation rebuilding, but whether the central thrust of Luther's reforming philosophy and activity was in fact antithetical to scholarship and the promotion of learning through books and libraries. Do the four arguments presented in the previous section validate Erasmus' contention that Lutheranism and the downfall of learning go together?

Little need be said concerning the book-burning ceremony at Wittenberg. The act was, of course, symbolic and did not imply a systematic campaign to rid the earth of papist literature. The materials committed to the flames were representative of the main theological issues at stake: the bull of excommunication (whether the pope had a right thus to deal with Luther's criticisms of the church),[15] compendiums of canon law (whether legal structure should be permitted to obscure and nullify the Gospel, as Luther believed it was doing in the case of indulgences), a common handbook for confessors (whether man's penitential, legalistic works ought to have more ultimate significance than God's free act of forgiveness in Jesus Christ), and typical scholastic refutations of Luther.[16] That the ceremony at the Elster gate was not an attempt at systematically destroying medieval theological literature is evident from the fact that the

---

[15] On throwing the *Exsurge Domine* bull into the fire, Luther said: "Because thou hast destroyed the truth of the Lord, the Lord consume thee in this fire" (Perlbach and J. Luther, *op. cit.*; Kawerau, *op. cit.*).

[16] The motivations behind the burning of these particular works are well presented by Heinrich Boehmer, *Martin Luther: Road to Reformation,* trans. J. W. Doberstein and T. G. Tappert (New York: Living Age Books, 1957), pp. 376-79.

works of Aquinas and Scotus, though representing great scholastis syntheses, were considered too valuable even for individual copies to be burned.[17] It is worth noting also that the Elster gate incident had been preceded by similar symbolic burnings of Luther's own writings.[18] These prior burnings do not make Luther's action more palatable, but they clearly demonstrate that the reformer was following well-established custom and not creating precedent. A useful parallel perhaps exists in the case of political burnings in effigy in our own day; surely these are not ceremonies to be encouraged, for they imply a low conception of human worth, but neither are they tantamount to murder.

The argument that a predestination theology tends to produce intellectual and cultural narrowness and quietism cannot be supported historically. The best illustration of this is probably provided by Erasmus and Calvin — Erasmus, the erstwhile defender of humanistic freedom of the will, and Calvin, the archpredestinarian. Max Weber, R. H. Tawney, and others have (for all their overstatement of the case) shown how activistic Calvin and his followers actually were in economic and cultural life; and the contrast with the introspective, hypochondriacal Erasmus could hardly be greater. Much the same contrast existed between Luther and Erasmus, and, as we shall see shortly, Luther did far more for the practical promotion of schools and

---

[17] Grisar, *op. cit.,* II (London: Kegan Paul, 1913), 51.

[18] While the bull of excommunication was being executed at Rome, Luther's books, together with a wooden statue of him, were publicly committed to the flames in the Piazza Navona (June 12, 1520); see Paul Kalkoff, "Zu Luthers römischen Prozess," *Zeitschrift für Kirchengeschichte,* XXV (1904), 129-30; cf. E. G. Schwiebert, *Luther and His Times* (St. Louis: Concordia Publishing House, 1950), p. 492. Luther's prince, Frederick the Wise, wrote as follows to one of the imperial counselors: "After I left Cologne, Luther's books were burned, and again at Mainz. I regret this . . . and I have constantly insisted that he should not be condemned unheard, nor should his books be burned. If now he has given tit for tat, I hope that His Imperial Majesty will graciously overlook it" (*SL* [St. Louis edition of Luther's works, ed. Walch], XV, No. 519); cf. Roland H. Bainton, *Here I Stand* (New York: Mentor Books, 1955), p. 129. Ceremonial book burnings should be carefully distinguished from systematic attempts to rid an area of heretical literature by collecting and burning it — a common practice of the Inquisition, especially in Italy and Spain (see George Haven Putnam, *The Censorship of the Church of Rome* [2 vols.; New York: Putnam, 1906-7], I, 13-14; II, 314 ff.; and *passim*).

libraries than did the prince of humanists.[19] As for Luther's
statements with regard to the relative unimportance of theological
books when compared with the Bible, we must see that this
position was based not on an obscurantist Biblicism, but on the
very humanist scholarship which Erasmus best represented: the
humanist had stressed the vital importance of the sources
(*fontes*) over against the bulk of secondary theological works,
and it is in this light that Luther criticizes the works of the doctors (and includes his own works in the criticism!). The reformer does not say that medieval theological productions are
of no value (he himself had studied them in the course of obtaining his doctorate in the Holy Scripture — the highest academic
degree in his day); he says rather that in selecting books distinctions must be made according to intrinsic value. The trouble,
as he saw it, was not that libraries contained scholastic literature,
but that "men have begun to pick up, *without any distinction in
particular,* all sorts of fathers, councils, and doctors." It was no
sufferer from intellectual myopia or bibliophobia who could write:
"Printing is the highest and ultimate gift of God,"[20] and, "There
never yet have been, nor are there now, too many good books."[21]
Although it is quite evident that "Luther could never think of
himself as a scholar in the way Erasmus did," for "he never
could share the Dutchman's confidence in the saving power of
sheer enlightenment, the grace of knowledge," yet one must also
recognize that "the truest way . . . to describe the beginning of
the Reformation is to say that it originated in *a scholar's insight,*
born equally of spiritual struggle and hard intellectual labor."[22]

The first decade of the Reformation was indeed marked by
a deterioration in educational institutions (both Roman Catholic

---

[19] Cf. Lester K. Born's accurate description of Erasmus' personality:
"Erasmus was not a man of the people, as was his contemporary and later
controversialist Martin Luther; nor did he have an intimate feeling for the
people. His concern for them (which was not unqualified) seems rather to
be in the attitude of one who sees from a position aloof, and not that of one
who has been a fellow-sufferer. By his very nature and constitution he was
removed from the coarser phases of life and unable to endure or to tolerate
them" (Lester K. Born [ed.], *The Education of a Christian Prince by Desi-
derius Erasmus* ["Columbia University Records of Civilization," No. 27;
(New York: Columbia University Press, 1936)], p. 19).

[20] *TR,* 1038. See Otto Clemen's excellent essay, *Luthers Lob der Buch-
druckerkunst* (Zwickau, Sachsen: Johannes Hermann, n.d.).

[21] *WA,* LIV, 3 (from Luther's 1543 preface to Wenzeslaus Link's *Annota-
tions on the Pentateuch*).

[22] E. Harris Harbison, *The Christian Scholar in the Age of the Reformation* (New York: Chas. Scribner's Sons, 1956), pp. 121, 123 (Harbison's
italics).

and Protestant), and this deterioration resulted, at least in part, from the chaotic social conditions produced by religious upheaval. However, to leave the story at this point would hardly be fair, and the best historians have been careful to present a better-rounded picture. In the first place, the initial decline in university enrolments cannot be laid entirely at Luther's door, for it "was due to a number of factors which affected all the German universities: discouragement of begging, which had formerly helped support students; reaction against humanism's artificial enthusiasm for formal education; insistence on the part of some religious radicals that manual labor is preferable to study; and the effects of the Peasant's War and recurring pestilence."[23] In the second place, Luther and his fellow reformers were acutely conscious of the seriousness of the educational situation in the 1520's, and dealt with it with remarkable effectiveness on all levels. Even during the worst of the decline, Luther's Wittenberg maintained higher enrolments than any other German university, Protestant or Catholic; and Luther's new educational pattern of Biblical humanism there came to be widely copied at such other German universities as Jena, Halle, and Erlangen. Indeed, "the transformation of Wittenberg marked the disappearance of the medieval university and the emergence of the first modern university of Germany and of the western world."[24]

In 1530, Luther took an unequivocal stand for compulsory public education,[25] and "this was not just a matter of paper resolves. If one applies modest standards, one can only wonder at how quickly the Reformation approached its goal. By the end of the sixteenth century in Germany a number of territories, Saxony, Hesse, Württemberg, had a flourishing public school system."[26] In this task Luther's co-worker Philipp Melanchthon performed inestimable service, and earned the designation "pre-

---

[23] Theodore G. Tappert, "Luther in His Academic Role," in *The Mature Luther,* ed. Gerhard L. Belgium ("Martin Luther Lectures," III [Decorah, Iowa: Luther College Press, 1959]), p. 42.

[24] E. G. Schwiebert, "New Groups and Ideas at the University of Wittenberg," *Archiv für Reformationsgeschichte,* XLIX, No. 1/2 (1958), 78.

[25] "I hold that it is the duty of the government to compel its subjects to keep their children in school" ("On Keeping Children in School" [1530], in *WA,* XXX, Pt. 2, 586).

[26] Karl Holl, *The Cultural Significance of the Reformation,* trans. Hertz and Lichtblau (New York: Living Age Books, 1959), pp. 111-12.

ceptor of Germany."[27] F. V. N. Painter's summary statement concerning Luther's educational contribution is a balanced one:

> In a few years the Protestant portion of Germany was supplied with schools. They were still defective in almost every particular; but, at the same time, they were greatly superior to any that had preceded them. Though no complete system of popular instruction was established, the foundation for it was laid. To this great result Luther contributed more than any other man of his time; and this fact makes him the leading educational reformer of the sixteenth century.[28]

In the matter of library losses during the Reformation, one must in fairness note that, generally speaking, the destruction of monastic collections took place not at the hands of the Lutherans, but at the hands of so-called "leftwing" reformers such as Carlstadt, and in the excesses of the peasant rebellions of the early sixteenth century. Instead of wanting the monasteries destroyed, Luther wished them to be converted into schools.[29] Moreover, he opposed Carlstadt and the peasants in such ve-

---

[27] See Karl Hartfelder, *Philipp Melanchthon als Praeceptor Germaniae* ("Monumenta Germaniae paedagogica," VII [Berlin: A. Hofmann, 1889]); James William Richard, *Philipp Melanchthon, the Protestant Preceptor of Germany* (New York: G. P. Putnam's Sons, 1898), and Clyde L. Manschreck, *Melanchthon, the Quiet Reformer* (New York: Abingdon Press, 1958). Cf. also the recent Melanchthon issue of the *Archiv für Reformationsgeschichte*, LI, No. 2 (1960), and Vilmos Vajta (ed.), *Luther and Melanchthon* (Philadelphia: Muhlenberg Press, 1961).

[28] *A History of Education* (New York: Appleton, 1886), p. 147. On the educational impact of Luther's reformation, see Harold J. Grimm, "Luther and Education," in *Luther and Culture*, ed. Gerhard L. Belgum ("Martin Luther Lectures," IV [Decorah, Iowa: Luther College Press, 1960]), pp. 71-142; and R. R. Caemmerer, "The Contributions of Lutheranism to Education, with Special Reference to Germany and the Scandinavian Countries," and O. J. Beyers, "The Impact of Lutheran Education on American Culture," both in *Proceedings of the First Institute on the Church and Modern Culture*, ed. John G. Kunstmann (Valparaiso, Ind., 1953), pp. 39-59.

[29] "I wish they would not tear apart the great monasteries, which without having the episcopal title are almost like dioceses. They should rather be turned into schools wherever such schools are needed" ("How To Install a Truly Christian Bishop," 1542; in *WA*, LIII, 255). Cf. George W. Forell, *Faith Active in Love: An Investigation of the Principles Underlying Luther's Social Ethics* (Minneapolis: Augsburg Publishing House, 1959), pp. 107-8.

hement language[30] that he has been severely criticized for it by his opponents — and yet it is often these same opponents who imply that he condoned or was responsible for the excesses of the Reformation. But Luther and his movement did not merely oppose the destruction of already-existing libraries; they engaged actively in the building of new libraries, as can be seen both on the university level and on the level of the lower schools.

The studies of E. G. Schwiebert[31] have shown that a furor of library activity went on at Wittenberg during Luther's professorship there. His close friend and fellow reformer, Georg Spalatin, served as librarian of the ducal university library, and made regular trips to Venice to buy Hebrew and Greek manuscripts needed by the Wittenberg faculty. "The many casual references in the correspondence of the period indicate that Spalatin, Melanchthon, Chancellor Brueck, and possibly several professors were constantly on the alert for new collections, such as those of Duke George, Aurogallus, and Hassenstein, and that a close supervision was kept over the fairs at Leipzig and Nuernberg in the search for choice volumes."[32] The breadth of content in the library belies any criticism of the Wittenberg reformers as narrow Biblicists: "The fact that the classics, and the Church Fathers, and the humanists were so well represented seems to point conclusively to the fact that the Reformers valued and employed Renaissance tools in the restoration of early Christianity.[33]

---

[30] Cf. E. Gordon Rupp, "Luther and Carlstadt," and "Luther and Thomas Müntzer," both in *Luther Today*, ed. Gerhard L. Belgum ("Martin Luther Lectures," I [Decorah, Iowa: Luther College Press, 1957]), pp. 107-46. It is of more than routine interest that Luther first became aware of the unrestrained violence of the peasant rebellions when in 1525 Melanchthon, Agricola, and he travelled to Eisleben to establish a new Christian school at the request of Count Albert of Mansfield; directly on his return home he wrote his well-known tract *Against the Murderous and Plundering Bands among the Peasants* (see Luther's *Briefwechsel*, ed. Ernst Ludwig Enders *et al.*, V [Calw and Stuttgart: Vereinsbuchhandlung, 1893], 157; and cf. Schwiebert, *Luther and His Times*, pp. 564-65).

[31] "Remnants of a Reformation Library," *Library Quarterly*, X (October, 1940), 494-531; Schwiebert, *Luther and His Times*, pp. 244-53.

[32] *Luther and His Times*, p. 253.

[33] Schwiebert, "Remnants of a Reformation Library," *op. cit.*, p. 530. On the Wittenberg library and Luther and Melanchthon's connection with it, see also Carl G. Brandis, "Luther und Melanchthon als Benutzer der Wittenberger Bibliothek," *Theologische Studien und Kritiken*, XC (1917), 206-21 (cf. Willi Göber, "Aus Melanchthons Bibliothek," *Zentralblatt für Bibliothekswesen* XLV [1928], 297-302), and E. Hildebrandt, "Die kurfürstliche Schloss- und Universitätsbibliothek zu Wittenberg, 1512-1547: Beiträge zu ihrer Geschichte," *Zeitschrift für Buchkunde*, II (1925), 34-42, 109-29, 157-88.

Et patris, & patrui, famam, virtutibus, æquat.
Qui patris & patrui, nobile nomen habet.
Adferit, inuicto diuinum pectore verbum,
Et Musas omni dexteritate iuuat.
Hinc etiam ad promptos studiorum contulit vsus,
Inspicis hoc præsens quod modo Lector opus.

CRANACH BOOKPLATE FOR WITTENBURG UNIVERSITY LIBRARY

In the educational efforts of the early Lutheran reformers, schools and libraries went hand in hand. The concern for establishing suitable book collections is evident not only in many of the visitation articles and agenda drawn up during the period,[34] but also and especially in the formal *Kirchenordnungen*,[35] drafted chiefly under the influence of Melanchthon (for central and southern Germany) and Johannes Bugenhagen (for northern Germany). In the work of Bugenhagen — like Melanchthon a colleague of Luther at Wittenberg — bibliothecal concern is particularly evident.[36] The following typical *Kirchenordnungen* regulations are the product of his influence:

> A library shall be erected not far from the school and the lecture hall, wherein all books, good and bad, which shall be acquired for this purpose in this city, shall be assembled; they shall be arranged in orderly manner, especially the best, each near others of its kind; keys thereto, one or four, should be in the hands of some, *viz.*, the rector and sub-rector and superintendent, that no damage may be done.[37]

---

[34] See Emil Sehling (ed.), *Die evangelischen Kirchenordnungen des XVI. Jahrunderts* (5 vols.; Leipzig: Reisland, 1902-1913), *passim* (v. indexes under "Bibliothek," "Pfarrbibliothek," etc.)

[35] "While it is hardly possible to give a concise definition of that term (translated into English as church ordinances), the following statement will make clear the general nature of the material: *Kirchenordnungen* is the name given all those regulations, especially those issued by cities and sovereigns, by means of which the church regulations which had previously been given were modified according to Reformation ideas, and the newly developed church system was more fully organized" (Charles L. Robbins, *Teachers in Germany in the Sixteenth Century* ["Teachers College, Columbia University, Contributions to Education," No. 52 (New York: Teachers College, Columbia University, 1912)], p. 10). The allied term *Schulordnungen* refers to the school regulations usually embodied in the *Kirchenordnungen*.

[36] On him, see Hermann Hering, *Doktor-Pomeranus, Johannes Bugenhagen* ("Schriften des Vereins für Reformations-geschichte," No. 22 [Halle: M. Niemeyer, 1888]). In 1537 the sphere of Bugenhagen's activity was extended as far as Denmark, where he was called by the Danish king to reorganize the University of Copenhagen and the country's schools and churches along Lutheran lines. Zeeden has shown how great an influence Luther's personality and doctrine had on both Bugenhagen and Melanchthon (Ernst Walter Zeeden, *The Legacy of Luther,* trans. Ruth Mary Bethell [London: Hollis & Carter, 1954], pp. 10-18).

[37] "Van der librie," Hamburg Church Order of 1529; text in Sehling, *op. cit.,* V, 499-500. Bugenhagen was the author of the Hamburg Order of 1529; it was based in part upon his *Kirchenordnung* for Brunswick (1528), in which he specifically recommended the complete corpus of Augustine, Ambrose, and Jerome (*alle boeke Augustini, alle Ambrosii, alle Hieronymi*) for the church library (Aemilius Ludwig Richter [ed.], *Die evangelischen Kirchenordnungen des sechszehnten Jahrhunderts* [2 vols.; Wiemar: Verlag des Landes-Industriecomptoirs, 1846], I, 113). On Bugenhagen's 1528 Bruns-

The old useful books should be brought
together in the cities and kept safely in a library. The deacon of the treasury shall, as much
as possible, increase the library every year, especially with German Bibles and volumes of
Luther's works. The parish clergy shall pray
and exhort the people to increase the libraries
through legacies. The pastor and deacons shall
see to it that an inventory is made and the library assiduously guarded.[38]

The result of such regulations was the establishment of numerous church and school libraries — such as that at Calbe a.d.
Milde (the heritage of the first evangelical pastor there, Elias
Hoffman, Luther's Wittenberg *corrector*) and that at Eisleben
(begun by Kaspar Güttel, a friend of Luther's).[39] The Lutheran
blend of educational and bibliothecal concerns reached its zenith
in the person of Ernest the Pious (1601-75), duke of Gotha and
Altenburg, who was called "the ideal of a Christian prince" and
"the prince among pedagogues and the pedagogue among
princes"; not only did he found the magnificent ducal library of
Gotha,[40] but he also, in the process of rebuilding his duchy from
the devastation of the Thirty Years' War, created "the best
type of school system organized in German lands before the late

wick Order were also based in part his Lübeck Order of 1531, the Soest Order
of 1532, the Bremen Order of 1534, his Pomerania Order of 1535, and his
Brunswick-Wolfenbüttel Order of 1543 — all of which contain library provisions (Richter, *op. cit.*, I, 146, 167-68, 243, 254; II, 61; Milkau and Leyh,
op. cit., III, Pt. 1, 560-62; Robbins, *op. cit.*, pp. 15-17, 43). The Pomerania
Kirchenordnung of 1535 directs that "a public library" be established in the
cities "for pastors, preachers, schoolmasters and assistant teachers, etc."
(*eyne gemeyne Liberie . . . vör de Parners, Predikers, Scholmesters unde
Scholgesellen, etc.*), and the Brunswick-Wolfenbüttel Order of 1543 has similar import (Richter [ed.], *op. cit.*, I, 254; II, 61). Monetary provisions for
book purchases are included in the Hesse Order of 1537 (*ibid.*, I, 284-85).
Cf. also the Lauenburg Order of 1585 (Sehling [ed.], *op. cit.*, V, 422, 427-28),
and the Danzig Order of 1612 (*ibid.*, IV, 201).

[38] "Van liberien," in Sec. V of the Pomeranian Church Orders of 1563 and
1569, based upon Bugenhagen's Pomeranian *Kirchenordnung* of 1535 (text
in Sehling [ed.], *op. cit.*, IV, 406; cf. p. 416).

[39] See the list in Milkau and Leyh (eds.), *op. cit.*, III, Pt. 1, 562, based
upon G. Kohfeldt, "Zur Geschichte der Büchersammlungen und des Büch-
erbesitzes in Deutschland," *Zeitschrift für Kulturgeschichte*, VII (1900),
354 ff. Cf. also O. Radlach, "Die Bibliotheken der evangelischen Kirche und ihre
rechtsgeschichtliche Entwicklung," *Zentralblatt für Bibliothekswesen*, XII
(1895), 153-73.

[40] Milkau and Leyh (eds.), *op. cit.*, III, Pt. 1, 626-37.

eighteenth century."[41] His *Schulmethode* of 1642 — "the pedagogic masterpiece of the seventeenth century"[42] — provided for universal, compulsory school attendance and for the preparation and free distribution of school books to all pupils. As a result, it was said that "Duke Ernest's peasants were better educated than noblemen anywhere else."

Thus, the Lutheran reform can hardly be treated as anti-cultural, anti-intellectual, or anti-bibliophilistic; the weight of evidence, in fact, points exactly in the other direction. But is it possible to argue, as Matthew Arnold did, that the academic accomplishments of the Lutheran Reformation were due not to Luther, but to his colleagues, since all the reformers of the first rank were eminent humanists with "the great but single exception" of Luther himself?[43] Such an interpretation has been called into serious question by the preceding discussion. Luther's great manifesto on the establishment of libraries shows how fallacious it actually is with regard to Reformation library activity.

THE BASIC LIBRARY PROMOTION DOCUMENT OF THE REFORMATION

The Luther research movement, which took its origin in recent years largely from Karl Holl's work, and which has produced "a veritable Luther-renaissance"[44] in our understanding of the reformer, has been based on two cardinal principles: first, Luther must be allowed to speak for himself, not through the mouths of later interpreters, whether friend or foe; and second, the touchstone in Luther interpretation must be the reformer's central convictions, not his occasional remarks, which, when taken in isolation from his central convictions, can be used to build utterly perverse and misleading descriptions of his character. In line with this approach, Luther's concern for library promotion is demonstrated by quoting at length from his great educational treatise of 1524, "To the Councilmen of All Cities in Germany, That They Establish and Maintain Christian Schools." Of this document Painter has said: "If we consider its pioneer character, in connection with its statement of principles and admirable

---

[41] Ellwood P. Cubberley, *Readings in the History of Education* (Boston: Houghton Mifflin Co., 1920), p. 252.

[42] Ellwood P. Cubberley, *The History of Education* (Boston: Houghton Mifflin Co., 1920), p. 317.

[43] Matthew Arnold, quoted in Harry G. Good, "The Position of Luther upon Education," *op. cit.*, p. 516.

[44] Wilhelm Pauck, in his Introduction to Holl, *op. cit.*, p. 12.

recommendations, the address must be regarded the most important educational treatise ever written."[45]

This treatise, which served as a basic mandate for all the Lutheran educational reforms discussed in the previous section, consists of thirty-three duodecimo pages in English translation, and of these no less than five full pages — the concluding five pages — are devoted to the establishment of libraries.[46] Because this document so fully expresses Luther's philosophy of library promotion, and because the treatise, which is of such importance to the history of government-supported libraries, has never been made directly available to readers of library literature, we shall transcribe at length its closing section. After doing so, we shall conclude with a brief analysis of the factors which led Luther to this powerful statement in behalf of establishing libraries.

> Finally, this must be taken into consideration by all who earnestly desire to see . . . schools established and the languages preserved in the German states: that no cost nor pains should be spared to procure good libraries in suitable buildings, especially in the large cities, which are able to afford it. For if a knowledge of the Gospel and of every kind of learning is to be preserved, it must be embodied in books, as the prophets and apostles did, as I have already shown. This should be done, not only that our spiritual and civil leaders may have something to read and study, but also that good books may not be lost, and that the arts and languages may be preserved, with which God has graciously favored us. St. Paul was diligent in this matter, since he lays the injunction upon Timothy: "Give attendance to reading"; and directs him to bring the books, but especially the parchments left at Troas.

---

[45] Painter, *op. cit.*, p. 143.

[46] I refer to and subsequently quote F. V. N. Painter's translation of this document, in his *Luther on Education* (St. Louis: Concordia Publishing House, 1928), pp. 203-8. (Permission to quote granted by the publisher.) Original text in *WA*, XV, 9-53. An English translation by A. T. W. Steinhaeuser appears in *PE* (the Philadelphia English language edition of Luther's works), IV, 101-3.

All the kingdoms that have been distinguished in the world have bestowed care upon this matter, and particularly the Israelites, among whom Moses was the first to begin the work, who commanded them to preserve the book of the law in the ark of God, and put it under the care of the Levites, that any one might procure copies from them. He even commanded the king to make a copy of this book in the hands of the Levites. Among other duties, God directed the Levitical priesthood to preserve and attend to the books. Afterwards Joshua increased and improved this library, as did subsequently Samuel, David, Solomon, Isaiah, and many kings and prophets. Hence have come to us the Holy Scriptures of the Old Testament, which would not otherwise have been collected and preserved, if God had not required such diligence in regard to it.

After this example the collegiate churches and convents formerly founded libraries, although with few good books. And the injury resulting from the neglect to procure books and good libraries, when there were men and books enough for that purpose, was afterwards perceived in the decline of every kind of knowledge; and instead of good books, the senseless, useless, and hurtful books of the monks, the *Catholicon, Florista, Graecista, Labyrinthus, Dormi Secure,*[47] and the like were introduced by Satan, so that the Latin language was corrupted, and neither good schools, good instruction, nor good methods of study remained. And as we see, the languages and arts are, in an imperfect manner, recovered from fragments of old books rescued from the worms and dust; and every day men are seeking these literary remains, as people dig in the ashes of a ruined city after treasures and jewels.

---

[47] The *Catholicon* (1286) was a Latin grammar and dictionary compiled by the Dominican monk Balbi of Genoa (Joannes Januensis); the *Florista,* a rhymed Latin syntax (1317) by Ludolf of Luchow, a canon of Hildesheim; the *Graecista,* or *Graecismus,* a poem on grammar, written in hexameters

Therein we have received our just due, and God has well recompensed our ingratitude, in that we did not consider His benefits, and lay up a supply of good literature when we had time and opportunity, but neglected it, as if we were not concerned. He in turn, instead of the Holy Scriptures and good books, suffered Aristotle and numberless pernicious books to come into use, which only led us further from the Bible. To these were added the progeny of Satan, the monks and the phantoms of the universities, which we founded at incredible cost, and many doctors, preachers, teachers, priests and monks, that is to say, great, coarse, fat asses, adorned with red and brown caps, like swine led with a golden chain and decorated with pearls; and we have burdened ourselves with them, who have taught us nothing useful, but have made us more and more blind and stupid, and as a reward have consumed all our property, and filled all the cloisters, and indeed every corner, with the dregs and filth of their unclean and noxious books, of which we can not think without horror.

Has it not been a grievous misfortune that a boy has hitherto been obliged to study twenty years or longer, in order to learn enough miserable Latin to become a priest and to read the mass? And whoever has succeeded in this, has been called blessed, and blessed the mother that

interspersed with elegiacs by Eberhard of Bethune (*fl.* 1212); the *Labyrinthus,* a poem on the miseries of teachers of rhetoric and poetry, reputedly by Eberhard of Bethune; the *Dormi secure* ("Sleep soundly"), a collection of sermons made by Johann von Werden (mid-fifteenth century) to reduce the anxieties of preachers by providing them with ready-made homilies. Balbi's knowledge of Greek is so slight that he derives the late Latin word *laicus* ("layman/member of the congregation") from the Greek λᾶας ("stone"), "for he is insensible and opaque to learning"; Ludolf's *Florista* is satirized by Erasmus in his *Conflictus Thaliae,* Act II; the *Graecismus,* mentioned by Swift in his *Battle of the Books,* owes its name to the fact that it contains a chapter on derivations from the Greek (a chapter demonstrating appalling ignorance of the language); the *Labyrinthus,* in its section on poetical literary criticism, omits Horace entirely, but includes among some thirty models of style "modern" Latin poets such as Petrus Riga and Alanus ab Insulis! On Balbi, Ludolf, and Eberhard, see John Edwin Sandys, *A History of Classical Scholarship,* I (3d ed.; Cambridge: Cambridge University Press, 1921), 554-55, 606, 616, 647, 666-68, 677.

has borne such a child! And yet he has remained a poor ignorant man all through life, and has been of no real service whatever. Everywhere we have had such teachers and masters, who have known nothing themselves, who have been able to teach nothing useful, and who have been ignorant even of the right methods of learning and teaching. How has it come about? No books have been accessible but the senseless trash of the monks and sophists. How could the pupils and teachers differ from the books they studied? A jackdaw does not hatch a dove, nor a fool make a man wise. That is the recompense of our ingratitude, in that we did not use diligence in the formation of libraries, but allowed good books to perish, and bad ones to survive.

But my advice is, not to collect all sorts of books indiscriminately, thinking only of getting a vast number together. I would have discrimination used, because it is not necessary to collect the commentaries of all the jurists, the productions of all the theologians, the discussions of all the philosophers, and the sermons of all the monks. Such trash I would reject altogether, and provide my library only with useful books; and in making the selection, I would advise with learned men.

In the first place, a library should contain the Holy Scriptures in Latin, Greek, Hebrew, German, and other languages. Then the best and most ancient commentators in Greek, Hebrew, and Latin.

Secondly, such books as are useful in acquiring the languages, as the poets and orators, without considering whether they are heathen or Christian, Greek or Latin. For it is from such works that grammar must be learned.

Thirdly, books treating of all the arts and sciences.

Lastly, books on jurisprudence and medicine, though here discrimination is necessary.

A prominent place should be given to chronicles and histories, in whatever languages they may be obtained; for they are wonderfully useful in understanding and regulating the course of the world, and in disclosing the marvelous works of God. O how many noble deeds and wise maxims produced on German soil have been forgotten and lost, because no one at the time wrote them down; or if they were written, no one preserved the books: hence we Germans are unknown in other lands, and are called brutes that know only how to fight, eat and drink. But the Greeks and Romans, and even the Hebrews, have recorded their history with such particularity, that even if a woman or child did any thing noteworthy, all the world was obliged to read and know it; but we Germans are always Germans, and will remain Germans.

Since God has so graciously and abundantly provided us with art, scholars, and books, it is time for us to reap the harvest and gather for future use the treasures of these golden years.

THE SOURCE OF LUTHER'S BIBLIOTHECAL CONCERN

It is a bit surprising at first glance that Luther, the prime figure in a great revolutionary movement, should have been so concerned to establish libraries — repositories which inevitably place a high value upon the past. One would expect that Luther, like Carlstadt, would have been the prototype of "the bloody-eyed anarchist who wants to tear the vines right off the buildings."[48] What brought Luther to his conviction that book collections were so important that they should be governmentally supported? The answer does not lie simply in the academic orientation of the professor-reformer (though it is significant that Luther always considered history to be the most valuable discipline outside of theology[49]); nor does the problem find its solu-

---

[48] E. B. White's description of a Cornell student type of his day (Hendrik Willem van Loon *et al.*, *Our Cornell* [Ithaca, N.Y.: Cornell Alumni Association, 1939], p. 10).

[49] "Historians are the most useful people and the best teachers, and they cannot be sufficiently honored, praised, and thanked" (Preface to Capella's History, 1538; in *WA*, I, 384). Cf. Heinrich Bornkamm, *Luther's World of Thought*, trans. Martin H. Bertram (St. Louis: Concordia Publishing House, 1958), pp. 195-217 ("God and History").

tion in that streak of conservatism in Luther's character which consistently led him to purify rather than initiate[50] and to oppose those who equated change with progress.[51] Luther's attitude towards books and libraries stemmed — as did all of his judgments — from his central convictions; in many ways he was a "man with one sermon," and we must go to his theological orientation for the source of his bibliothecal concern.[52]

Luther's major objection to the theology and practical piety of the church of his day was that it led man to false security or to despair by centering attention on human effort to achieve salvation. Through agonizing personal experience as a monk, and through careful study of the Biblical sources as a university lecturer, Luther came to the conclusion that it was folly for man to try to bridge the gulf between his fallible humanity and God's perfect holiness, and that this was not in fact expected of him at all, for God had himself done everything necessary for man's salvation. Thus Luther wrote in the Ninety-five Theses: "The true treasure of the Church is the Most Holy Gospel of the glory and the grace of God."[53] But what precisely had God done for man's salvation? He had given his *Word* to man. And what is this Word? In the fullest sense, Jesus Christ — the Λόγος of the Gospel writer (John 1) — the Divine Self-Communication, who "redeemed me, a lost and condemned creature, delivered and freed me from all sins, from death, and from the power of the devil, not with silver and gold but with his holy and precious blood and with his innocent sufferings and death."[54] This Word

[50] Liturgically, e.g., "Luther protested against unevangelical features but never sought to abolish the historic order and substitute a new service built upon evangelical principles. . . . He was convinced that purification and not destruction was needed" (Luther D. Reed, *The Lutheran Liturgy* [Philadelphia: Muhlenberg Press, 1947], p. 68).

[51] "To change is easy, to improve is troublesome and dangerous" (*WA*, XIX, 639). Cf. George W. Forell, "Luther and Politics," in *Luther and Culture*, pp. 42-43.

[52] "Luther's interest in primary and secondary schools stems primarily from his overwhelming religious concern. Recent Luther scholarship has established beyond a doubt that the Reformation had its origins in Luther's inner struggle concerning salvation" (Grimm, "Luther and Education," in *Luther and Culture*, p. 76). In this regard see especially Gerhard Ritter, *Die Weltwirkung der Reformation* (2d ed.; Munich: R. Oldenbourg, 1959), pp. 44-45.

[53] Thesis 62 (*PE*, I, 35). See Philip S. Watson, *Let God Be God! An Interpretation of the Theology of Martin Luther* (London: Epworth Press, 1947).

[54] Luther, "Small Catechism," Pt. II, Art. 2 (in *The Book of Concord*, trans. and ed. Theodore G. Tappert *et al.* [Philadelphia: Muhlenberg Press, 1959], p. 345). See also Luther's "Treatise on Christian Liberty" (1520), in *PE*, II, 315.

was made the focus of attention in Luther's great Reformation hymn, *Ein' Feste Burg*. Singing his defiance of Satan and all his minions, Luther wrote:

One little Word o'erthrows him.

Christ the Word now comes to men through the Word preached about him (the Gospel), and through the written Word (the Bible) in which the Good News is recorded historically. A book thus becomes a "means of grace," and the only final check upon Christian doctrines, teachings, and practice. Luther had no patience with the "left-wing" reforming enthusiasts (*Schwärmer*) of his day, such as Thomas Müntzer, who felt that they were so completely led by God's Spirit that they could dispense with "book religion" and with the learning which had to accompany it. To Müntzer's cry of "Bible, Babel, bubble!" Luther answered that apart from God's written revelation he would not listen to Müntzer even if "he had swallowed the Holy Ghost, feathers and all."[55] Luther could say this because he believed that the Word is the tool of the Spirit — that the Spirit is given in, by, through, and with the Word.[56]

Thus the reading of the Bible, the study of the original languages of the Scriptures, and the collection of libraries became mandatory in Luther's program. The chain of reasoning was inescapable: To be saved a man has to believe in Christ the Word; to comprehend who Christ is, one must meet him in the preaching of the Gospel and in Holy Writ; and to understand what the Scriptures say, pastor and even layman cannot avoid the tools of scholarship.[57]

Certain corollaries of Luther's basic theological principle provided added motivation toward library establishment. The universal spiritual priesthood of believers was one such corollary. In his *Babylonian Captivity of the Church* (1520) Luther declared: "Let everyone . . . who knows himself to be a Christian

[55] *WA*, XVII, Pt. 1, 361-62.

[56] See Regin Prenter, *Spiritus Creator: Luther's Concept of the Holy Spirit*, trans. John M. Jensen (Philadelphia: Muhlenberg Press, 1953), p. 255 (see esp. the *WA* citations in n. 4) and *passim*.

[57] Cf. Pierce Butler (*op. cit.*, p. 80): "When the Reformation substituted truth for authority as the standard of orthodoxy the piety of the ecclesiastic was still measured by his assiduity in reading. But this was of a new sort: where his predecessor had been required to devote long daily hours to the perusal of a calendared breviary, the protestant minister was duty-bound to a lifelong self-directed exploration of serious literature. His work-room became a book-lined study instead of a sacristy."

be assured of this, and apply it to himself, that we are all priests, and there is no difference between us, that is to say, we have the same power in respect to the Word and all the sacraments."[58] In practice this view freed the layman from the legal demands of a priestly caste, but at the same time it placed a great personal responsibility on him. The matter of salvation could no longer be handled for one by a hierarchy; now, each man would have to confront the Word. Luther's monumental translation of the Bible into the German vernacular testifies to his conviction that the Bible must not be allowed to remain the property of a special class of believers.[59] Compulsory education, and municipal schools with libraries in conjunction with them, were thus essential for making the universal priesthood a practical reality.

Another corollary of Luther's doctrine of salvation by God's grace through faith was the conviction that "God, having no need for our works and benefactions for himself, bids us to do for our neighbor what we would do for God."[60] The man who thinks he can save himself, said Luther, will devote all his energies to placating God — and will probably seek the supposedly highest form of God-pleasing activity, monastic piety; but the result will be the misdirection of spiritual energy, for God wants us to serve our fellow men. But only the man who has had the core problem of his salvation taken care of by Jesus Christ is freed from personal anxiety and can direct his full energies to improve his neighbor's lot. The man who trusts in Christ can say: "I

---

[58] *PE*, II, 282-83 (cf. T. A. Kantonen, *Resurgence of the Gospel* [Philadelphia: Muhlenberg Press, 1948], pp. 158-70).

[59] See M. Reu, *Luther's German Bible* (Columbus, Ohio: Lutheran Book Concern, 1934). Cf. Holl, *op. cit.*, pp. 109-10: "That the Reformation concerned itself with higher culture at all and included cultural strivings among its goals from the beginning was already demanded by its religious point of origin. For it was indeed not an enthusiastic movement expecting its assurance of God through a direct bestowal of the spirit. Instead, by referring the individual to the Bible, a not inconsequential measure of knowledge, of examining something historically given, was included in the religious experience itself. And further, how should one be in a position to exercise the rights of the universal priesthood, i.e., to maintain his independent judgment in the highest ethical and religious questions, if he was not educated for this purpose? Not only was the education of the will necessary for this end, but also a universal education of the intellect. Everyone must at least be brought to the point where he could read the Bible and draw independent instruction from it. And as a support for this, the church had to possess systematic knowledge that could solve scholarly problems and give instruction in the disciplined use of the Bible."

[60] Fastenpostille (1525); in *WA*, XVII, 98. Cf. Forell, *Faith Active in Love*, chap. v ("The Ethical Principle"), pp. 70-111.

will give myself as a Christ to my neighbor, just as Christ offered himself to me."[61] This ethic of 'faith active in love" gave powerful social action motivation to Luther's work and led him to combat ignorance and illiteracy among his German people. For Luther establishment of libraries became in a real sense a fruit of faith.

A final corollary relevant to library promotion in Luther's thought was his belief in God's "two kingdoms." Luther did not see God as acting solely through his Gospel; to the reformer it was evident both from Scripture and from experience that God has an *opus alienum* ("strange work") as well as an *opus proprium* ("proper work"). God's "strange work" is His preserving activity whereby, through the structures of human existence such as the state and the family, He keeps human beings from destroying themselves in their sin. The Gospel, by its very nature, operates only in the hearts of Christians — and in them only insofar as they are Christians — but the Law (God's preserving work) forces all men to play God's masquerade.[62] In the realm of the created structures (*Schöpfungsordnungen*), reason, not faith, has to be exercised — and here the best schooling and the best knowledge of past human experience are called for.[63] Thus Luther's remarkable assertion concerning the need for men of highest caliber and training in politics: "There is need in this office of abler people than are needed in the office of preaching, so that it is necessary to keep the best boy for this work; for in the preaching office Christ does the whole thing, by His Spirit, but in the government of the world one must use reason — from

---

[61] "Treatise on Christian Liberty" (1520), in *PE*, II, 337.

[62] The connecting links between the two kingdoms are (1) the individual Christian, who lives in both realms simultaneously, since he is "justified and a sinner at the same time" (*simul justus et peccator*), and (2) the theological use of the Law, i.e., the ever accusing Law (*lex semper accusat*) which acts as a "schoolmaster to bring men to Christ." On Luther's doctrine of the two kingdoms and his distinction between Law and Gospel, see his *Commentary on Galatians* (1535), in *WA*, XL, Pt. 1, 46, 336-37, and *passim;* and cf. Gustaf Wingren, *Creation and Law*, trans. Ross Mackenzie (Edinburgh: Oliver & Boyd, 1961), and C. F. W. Walther, *The Proper Distinction between Law and Gospel*, ed. W. H. T. Dau (St. Louis: Concordia Publishing House, [1928]). The application of these principles to human interaction in society is well set forth in Wingren's *Luther on Vocation*, trans. Carl C. Rasmussen (Philadelphia: Muhlenberg Press, 1957).

[63] "Luther was the first educator in modern times to see the need for universal, compulsory education, not only because the basic principles of the Reformation made it necessary that all persons be able to read the Bible, but because both church and state required trained personnel" (Grimm, "Luther and Education," in *Luther and Culture*, p. 84).

which the laws have come — for God has subjected temporal rule and the affairs of the body to reason (Genesis 2:19) and has not sent the Holy Spirit from heaven for this purpose."[64] The consequence of this view was to give public schooling and municipal library promotion a vital role in both of God's "kingdoms" — to make them vital from the standpoint both of God's saving work in proclaiming the Word, and of His preserving work in sustaining human government, society, and culture.

Conclusion

The attempt has been made here to delineate the important position of Luther in the history of libraries. The study should be of value in demonstrating the inseparability of bibliographical history from general history,[65] and the utility of depth studies of historical personages who have contributed to bibliothecal development. Luther's concern for library promotion may also suggest revision of the old aphorism that "it matters little what you believe as long as you are sincere"; in the realm of books and libraries, as in all other realms, what one believes makes all the difference in the world as to what one does.

---

[64] "On Keeping Children in School," *op. cit.*, p. 562.

[65] Cf. Reinhold Niebuhr's pregnant assertion that "the fabric of history is woven upon one loom" ("The Unity of History," *Christianity and Crisis*, II [May 4, 1942], 1).

IV
LUTHER ON POLITICS
AND RACE

A. SHIRER'S RE-HITLERIZING OF LUTHER

B. A DAY IN EAST GERMAN LUTHER COUNTRY

A.

SHIRER'S RE-HITLERIZING
OF LUTHER

Credit for the first venture in publishing pocket-sized books should be given to Aldus Manutius, a Venetian printer of the High Renaissance, who sold numerous pocket editions of the Greek and Latin classics to a book-hungry Europe. In the past two decades of the present century the American book trade has been revolutionized by a new application of Manutius' principle: the paperbound, pocket-sized book distributed to an enormous public through retail magazine outlets. In an age of mass communication the mass-produced, mass-distributed "paperback" is a force to be reckoned with.

And it is a force with massive impact — both positive and negative. The ambivalent influence of the paperback is perhaps nowhere better indicated than in the case of William L. Shirer's *Rise and Fall of the Third Reich,* which, having been published in a ten-dollar, hard-cover edition (Simon & Schuster) in August 1960 and having enjoyed Book-of-the-Month Club promotion in November of that year, was forthwith issued in a paper-covered edition (Crest Book, Fawcett) in May, 1962. Its 1599 pages require a large pocket but a small pocketbook, and it has sold like the proverbial hotcakes in drug stores and on magazine counters throughout the United States and Canada. Moreover, its over-all quality — the *New York Times* reviewer called it "one of the most important works of history of our time" — and eminently readable style have brought about not only its purchase but also its careful perusal. The bookstore manager when I was at the University of Chicago, for example, set himself the task of reading the book in his morning coffee breaks; at the rate of two pages per day, he would have finished it in about three years!

But when our bookstore manager and the multitude of other readers arrived at pages 134-135 of Shirer's book, and more especially when they reached pages 326-328, they encountered an interpretation of the historical roots of the Third Reich which is highly misleading and harmful, for it sees in the father of Protestantism a prime source of nazi ideology. Amazingly, the thesis propounded in 1945 by Peter F. Wiener in his *Martin Luther: Hitler's Spiritual Ancestor* — and refuted with verve and erudition by Gordon Rupp (*Martin Luther — Hitler's Cause — or Cure?*) — has been resuscitated by Shirer and spread across a continent by the most efficient book distribution method yet discovered.

I

What, specifically, does Shirer contend with reference to Martin Luther? His discussion contains four criticisms, two of which he mentions in passing (Luther "employed a coarseness and brutality of language unequaled in German history until the Nazi time"; Luther's reform brought about a "disaster of religious differences") and two upon which he lays exceedingly heavy stress (as a "passionate" and "savage anti-Semite" and as a "ferocious believer in absolute obedience to political authority" Luther paved the way ideologically for the Third Reich). None of these arguments is new, but all of them assume new importance when advocated by an author of Shirer's reputation and influence. We shall consider each of these criticisms in turn, with special emphasis on the latter two.

From his own day to the present, Luther has often been pictured as a coarse and brutal man — as (to employ the phrase of a former colleague) a "wild bull of the theological pampas." On confronting his Ninety-Five Theses Leo X is supposed to have said, "These have been written by a drunken German." And the humanists of Luther's time, when they broke with him, frequently treated him as an uncultured, violent controversialist. Similarly, the contemporary humanist philosopher-historian Will Durant flatly asserts that Luther "was guilty of the most vituperative writing in the history of literature." It is true that Luther was of peasant stock and always retained the earthiness characteristic of his Saxon origin; but he was at the same time a scholar who earned the highest academic degree of his day (Doctor of the Sacred Scriptures), who spent his life as a university professor, and whose learning and cultural interests are beyond dispute. In actuality, Luther's literary "vulgarity" was not peculiar to him but was a common phenomenon of the time, and only by refusing to see Luther in historical context can Shirer's argument be sustained. As Roland Bainton has well pointed out: "Luther delighted less in muck than many of the literary men of his age. . . . Detractors have sifted from the pitch-blende of his ninety tomes a few pages of radioactive vulgarity."

The allegation that Luther is to be blamed for the "disaster of religious differences" resulting from the Reformation can be questioned on three grounds. First, a balanced picture of the condition of the Christian church at the beginning of the 16th century — a picture such as is painted by Myron Gilmore of Harvard in his *World of Humanism* — will show that the break-up of medieval unity had become virtually inevitable, and that in this respect Luther acted chiefly as a catalyst. Second, Luther did *not* pave the way for religious fragmentation by teaching "the supremacy of the individual conscience," as Shirer asserts; Luther held that individual conscience should be — as he said at the momentous Diet at Worms — "captive to the word of God," i.e., subject to the objective, perspicuous word of Christ. Thus Luther had little tolerance for the *Schwärmer* and other sectarians who wished to extend reforming activities on the basis of the internal protest of conscience. Third, even in our day of strong ecumenical conviction we must ask whether, in fact, religious differences are always "disastrous"; if, as Tillich claims, the "Protestant principle" requires that "expressions of the ultimate concern of the community must include their own criticism," then reformation and re-formation have a vital and continual part to play in the eternal protest against idolatry.

II

Far more important to Shirer's argument than the preceding criticisms is his charge that Luther was the forerunner of Hitlerian anti-Semitism and political absolutism. The claim that Luther was a "savage anti-Semite" is based largely upon his tract *Von den Juden and ihren Lügen* (1542),[1] written four years before his death. Indeed a violent pamphlet, reflecting the irritability that age and disease had brought upon Luther, its intent and message nonetheless have generally been misunderstood, and this is certainly true in Shirer's case. From *The Rise and Fall of the Third Reich* one would conclude that Luther passionately hated the Jewish race and believed that physical persecution was the proper means of dealing with it. However, as Bainton correctly emphasizes, Luther's position, unlike that of nazi Germany, "was entirely religious and in no respect racial."

Luther — and here his naiveté is certainly in evidence — could not understand why the Jews did not return to Christ after the errors of the papacy had been revealed and the Gospel purified; and, along with virtually all Christians of his time, Catholic as well as Protestant, he regarded all unbelievers as a positive social menace. Indeed, Luther "drew his material from medieval Catholic anti-Semite writings" (Rupp). But Luther did not resort to unthinking advocacy of persecution, as Shirer implies by his Luther quotations — taken, unhappily, out of context. Luther spoke not of depriving Jews of their wealth per se

---

[1] *Luthers Werke*, Weimarer Ausgabe, Bd. 53.

but of removing from them the wealth which they had unjustly obtained through usurious practice. And the confiscated monies were to be held in trust to be used for the maintenance of converted Jews —especially the "old and infirm" —according to their needs. Moreover, in order that the Jews might not continue to carry on their "sinful" financial practices, Luther proposed their return to Palestine, in line with the accepted principle of territorialism, or, failing that, their resumption of the vocation of agriculture (i.e., resumption of the more secure position they had enjoyed in the early medieval period).

Shirer does not quote the prefatory statement to Luther's proposals, which conveys the tone of his treatise: "We must indeed with prayer and the fear of God before our eyes exercise a keen compassion towards them and seek to save some of them from the flames. Avenge ourselves we dare not. Vengeance a thousand times more than we can wish them is theirs already." As Rupp says: "It all falls very far short of the Nazi anti-Semitism with its doctrine of Race, with its mass extermination, with its atrocities and with its inter-marriage laws." The basis of these horrifying practices was not the teachings of Luther; Jarman (*The Rise and Fall of Nazi Germany*) has shown that the nazi anti-Semitism actually "rested on the mystical feeling for German blood and soil and that the Jew polluted the blood" — a theory for which the philosopher Dühring and the composer Wagner were especially responsible.

Shirer also contends that Luther's condemnation of the peasant uprisings of 1524-1525 resulted in the "demeaning subservience" of the German people to political absolutism and in the easy acquiescence of their clergy to the Hitler regime. The erroneous nature of this oft-repeated assertion is apparent on several counts. First, Luther's strongly worded tract *Wider die räuberischen und mörderischen Rotten der Bauern*[2] was written in an honest effort to save the German lands from complete chaos. It followed personal efforts on Luther's part to bring the peasants to their senses; it included admonitions to the princes to go beyond strict duty in offering terms to the peasants; and when the tract was used by unscrupulous rulers as an excuse for wanton bloodshed, Luther followed it by another pamphlet (which Luther's critics seldom mention) wherein he declared that the devils, on leaving the peasants, had not returned to hell but had now entered the victorious and vengeful princes. Second,

---

[2] *Luthers Werke*, Weimarer Ausgabe, Bd. 18.

LUTHER PRESENTS WORD OF CHRIST TO PEASANTS

it is exceedingly unfair to claim that Luther advocated political totalitarianism, for, as George Forell has demonstrated in his *Faith Active in Love,* Luther "believed that the God of history must and will punish those [rulers] who trespass against his eternal moral law." Thus Heinrich Bornkamm (*Luther's World of Thought*) speaks only the plain truth when he says of Luther: "In the German nation he instilled an aversion to an absolute imperialism, an aversion not forgotten until very recent times, and then only by a relatively small number who were alienated from the Christian tradition."

Third, the attitude of the German Protestant clergy to Hitler was — except for the aberrational *Glaubensbewegung Deutscher Christen* — positive only at the outset, when any change from the miseries of the Weimar Republic seemed an improvement. As soon as the true character of the Third Reich became evident, the Protestant clergy (e.g., Martin Niemöller) opposed the regime to the limits of their ability. How far many of them went in what they thought was rendering unto God the things that are God's is seen in such a memorial volume as *Dying We Live: The Final Messages and Records of the Resistance.* Finally, the argument that in Luther one finds the basic root of nazi totalitarianism misses the real historical source of the Third Reich: the abnormally late development of a centralized German state. As Barraclough has shown in his *Origins of Modern Germany,* the German lands were condemned to weakness and decentralization as early as the "First Reich" (specifically, not later than the Hohenstaufen period — even before the Golden Bull of 1356), and until relatively recent times Germany suffered at the hands of such strongly centralized, aggressive, absolutist powers as the France of Louis XIV. Having acquired what might be termed a national inferiority complex, Germany in our time not unnaturally over-compensated for it by an attitude of arrogant superiority. The tragedy is that such a Germany became capable of imperialist expansion at a time when the science of armaments made conquest on a worldwide scale a live possibility. But for this Luther can hardly be held responsible.

III

Why, we may well ask, does as competent a student of history and of world affairs as William L. Shirer present the misleading view of Luther which has been analyzed here? The London *Times Literary Supplement* reviewer supplied a partial answer when he wrote in criticism of *The Rise and Fall of the Third Reich:*

> Luther was not the spiritual ancestor of Hitler. Nor can this particular label be affixed to Bismarck. To say that National Socialism was in the main stream of German historical development is to accept the claim which many Nazi writers put forward — men who were only too anxious to give some intellectual respectability to the weird hotchpotch of ideas which made up Nazi doctrine by citing the great names of Germany's past in their support.

Ironically, Shirer has been deceived by the nazi ideologists themselves. But the problem goes deeper than this. Shirer could not have remained thus deceived had he made the same effort to read the primary sources and the best critical scholarship on Luther as he did with respect to the Third Reich itself. The Luther sections of his book are entirely without documentation, but it is evident from a careful examination of his general sources that he derived his view of Luther from such negativistic secondary and tertiary materials as Roepke's *Solution of the German Problem* and A. J. P. Taylor's *Course of German History;* and these works show no acquaintance with the modern Luther-research movement, stemming from the work of Karl Holl, which in the last 40 years has revolutionized the interpretation of the Reformer's life and work. It is a real tragedy that Shirer has aided in the perpetuation of a view of Luther which is historically untenable and which seriously distorts Luther's real character and beliefs. The specter of a self-seeking, hate-inspired Antichrist patent to us in the Third Reich's rise and fall would have been even more evident to Luther, for the gravitational center of his theology and of his entire being was the true Christ, who, as the Reformer wrote in one of his Christmas hymns, "came to earth so mean and poor,/Man to pity and restore,/And make us rich in heaven above,/Equal with angels through His love."

B.

A DAY IN EAST GERMAN
LUTHER COUNTRY

My Strasbourg Th.D. dissertation was now in the hands of the three-man professorial jury who, in just nine days, would subject me to the centuries-old (but nonetheless appalling) public *soutenance* upon which the success of all my European academic labors depended. Exactly one week after the thesis defense my family and I would board the S.S. *France* for the return journey to America. Time was running out on a year of magnificence and wonder, and I had yet to fulfill one of the prime ambitions of the European sojourn: to see the places of Luther's major activity.

Of course we had travelled to the West-zone Luther towns of Marburg (where the Castle room still remains in which the Wittenberg Reformer chalked "Hoc est corpus meum," on the table to express disapproval of Zwingli's efforts to spiritualize the Lord's Supper) and Worms (where the magnificent Reformation memorial presents a stalwart Luther, Bible in hand, surrounded by such other advocates of reform as Hus, Savonarola, Peter Waldo, and Melanchthon). We had attempted to console ourselves for the lack of Western European Reformation sites by visiting Geneva's International Monument of the Reformation, which, curiously, contains statues only of those who contributed to the rise and spread of Calvinism. But these brief forays were unsatisfying at best: the chamber where the Marburg Colloquy took place has been entirely refurnished in replica, and photostats of documents in glass cases strike an incongruous note; Worms has long since lost to war the *Pfalz* near its Cathedral, where Luther refused to recant though the Holy Roman Emperor demanded it and his very life hung in the balance; and Geneva's stylized monument has uncomfortable architectural parallels with modern political hero-cult statues.

Nothing, in short, would serve as a satisfactory substitute for the Luther country of Saxony. I recalled the superlative article by the Welch novelist Gwyn Thomas in which he described his visit to Wittenberg and other East-German Luther sites; on seeing the *Schlosskirche* where Luther posted his Ninety-Five Theses, Thomas could not restrain himself from remarking, "Every nail he used to affix his documents to the wood went right through the heart and mind of Europe." ("Martin Luther: The New Piety," *Esquire,* January, 1964). How could I myself leave Europe without seeing such birthplaces of Protestantism? Moreover, what better time to go, since to remain in tranquil Strasbourg contemplating a not-so-tranquil thesis defense scheduled for the next week was hardly to my liking!

Adventure is an excellent counteractive for pre-examination syndrome, and closer contact with the courageous Luther might have empathic as well as historic benefit.

THE PROBLEM OF ENTREE

U.S. passports presently restrict American citizens from travelling in certain politically dangerous areas, e.g., China and Cuba. The "DDR" (Deutsche Demokratische Republik: East Germany) is not on the restricted list; however, since it is not recognized as a legitimate government by the United States, I anticipated some difficulties in travelling there. On inquiring at the U.S. Consulate in Strasbourg as to proper entrance procedures for East Germany, I was informed that, since I was pressed for time, the only possible procedure was to go to a border checkpoint and try to get a visa on the spot; and I was presented with an official consular mimeograph titled, "Information for Visitors to Berlin and the Soviet Zone of Germany." This document was evidently written to dissuade Americans from entering East Germany. "Such travel is not recommended except for compelling reasons," it said; and warning was given that "the signs you may see along the Zone borders are not warning that a person is approaching the border but mark the border itself, and to pass beyond them is to enter the Soviet Zone. They must not be disregarded. Frequent cases of arrest have occurred even when persons were only one or two feet inside the Soviet Zone."

Though the consular mimeograph did not convince me to stay at home (how is mutual understanding among peoples possible without communication?), it did cause me to make the trip alone, without my family. At about 11 A.M. on June 17, I crossed the Rhine from France into West Germany at Kehl, exchanged my francs for DM's (since parity is maintained between the West and East Germans marks), and pointed my Citroën ID 19 north toward the nearest appropriate East German checkpoint (Wartha, near Eisenach). My route took me over the Autobahn throughway system (Hitler's only positive contribution?), passing close to the wealthy gambling center of Baden-Baden, the industrial city of Karlsruhe, the famed Heidelberg of the *Student Prince,* and the centuries-old publishing center of Frankfurt am Rhein. Absence of speed limits on the Autobahn system made possible excellent mileage — even for a theologian — and by late afternoon I found myself at the West German Autobahn terminus. I passed onto a poorly paved road which continued for some twenty kilometers before reaching the border proper. (Having been intimidated by the consular mimeograph I slowed down for each of perhaps fifteen signs along this road — all of which, to my irritation, did *not* mark the border, but merely indicated that it was so-and-so many kilometers away!)

Finally, as the sun was setting, I arrived at the checkpoint. There ensued two hours of haggling on the visa problem with two minor officials whose genuine attempt to be helpful on the personal level was continually in tension with the rigidity of their bureaucratic ideology. "No, I could not obtain a scholar's visa without first going to the Educational and Cultural Bureau in Berlin." "I did not even want to visit East Berlin — only the Luther country? Really?" Finally (and not without difficulty, since the discussion strained my spoken German to the breaking point — neither official being able to speak either French or English), I persuaded them to trust me as a simple tourist, not as a visiting scholar-researcher, and to provide me with a day's visa on that basis.

Success! The officials were almost as happy as I to find a modus operandi, and after another half hour spent in preparing an unbelievable number of documents and in phoning ahead to Erfurt to establish hotel accomodations for the night (standard East German border procedure — to keep an eye on visitors!), the border police released me and my car for a day of travel to the sites of Luther's reforming activity. By the following midnight I would have to be back at the checkpoint. I resolved to take no chances — for whereas Cinderella had to face only a change from princess to servant girl at that hour, I might well encounter greater difficulties!

Erfurt: Hotel and Monastery

Soon, to my relief, the Autobahn resumed, though its East German portion was in serious disrepair as compared with the Western section. Nonetheless, I made good time, and by 23:30 (11:30 P.M.), I reached the Erfurter Hof, my hotel for the night. In finding it, I had to ask directions of several persons on the Erfurt streets; here I met a consistent phenomenon: whenever I introduced myself as an American, I was greeted with broad smiles of cordiality, coupled with the amazement I expect we in America would display on meeting a Martian! My car was examined with curiosity and some envy, and more than one person remarked that no cars of that quality were being made *here*.

The Erfurter Hof had obviously at one time been a hotel of considerable stature. The employees still made a valiant effort to retain the old tone, but cracking plaster and frayed carpets betrayed an economic system that simply did not encourage the niceties of life. In more ways than one it seemed that the hotel was trying to become a Wellsian time-machine for travel into a better past: late dancers in one ballroom were foxtroting to "Stardust" and other American pop music of the thirties, and a government chauffeur, who was taxiing a wealthy Italian matron through East Germany and with whom I ate a late snack, had a look of profound melancholy and nostalgia on his face when he told me that he could no longer himself visit any of the countries of Western Europe.

In the morning I spent an hour at the Augustinian Church and Cloister where Luther, after taking the M.A. at Erfurt University, had found monastic mysticism, work-righteousness, and scholasticism alike to be dead-ends of the spiritual life, and had turned to the God of a perspicuous Scripture whose Son died once for all to save to the uttermost those who trust solely in Him. In spite of unrepaired World War II bomb damage to the Cloister, the spirit of Luther's struggle touches the visitor deeply — perhaps more so because the present-day Church, now Evangelical, is evidently struggling so courageously to survive under a political regime which has rendered its economic situation close to penury.

WITTENBERG: THE CENTER OF LUTHER'S REFORM

The two-hundred-odd Autobahn kilometers from Erfurt to Wittenberg were covered in two hours. The route sped past Goethe's Weimar; Halle, where Wittenberg University survives today only in the composite name of "Wittenberg-Halle" University; and Leipzig, the renowned literary and academic center, the scene of the great debate in which Luther triumphed over his formidable opponent Johann Eck, while at the same time identifying himself with many of the "heretical" (yet Biblical) views of John Hus.

The town of Wittenberg has produced a negative first impression on all who have seen it — including Luther himself, who, like a 16th century Ogden Nash, wrote of it: "Little land, little land, You are but a heap of sand." To a present-day follower of the Reformation there is perhaps even more reason to look askance at the unimpressive little village that compares unfavorably with the great Leipzig near by; could one of the most significant movements in world history really have begun in such humble surroundings? Yet, on second glance, what should the Christian expect? Were the Jews a great people — to whom the oracles of God came? Was Bethlehem an influential metropolis? Were the apostles mighty men when chosen by our Lord? It seems to be a fundamental rule in the Divine operation to "choose the weak things of this world to confound the wise."

Wittenberg would have been nothing without Luther, and this applies today as much as it did in his own time (the official name of the town is now "Lutherstadt Wittenberg"). The town square is dominated by the two magnificent statues of Luther and Melanchthon erected in 1860. Just off the square is the Town Church, where Luther was married; in it is the younger Cranach's superlative Reformation Altarpiece, showing Luther and other Wittenberg Reformers seated around their Lord at the Last Supper, and, in another panel, Luther proclaiming Christ crucified to his congregation ("Other foundation can no man lay than that is laid, which is Jesus Christ").

Not far from the marketplace is the Castle Church, and what a numinous structure is that *Schlosskirche!* To stand before the tomb of Luther; to gaze at the portal where he posted the Theses on All Saints' Eve in 1517 (even though the original door has been replaced by a metal one carrying the theses in relief upon it!); to contemplate the statues of Jonas, Spalatin, and Brenz, who fought the good fight and kept the faith; to examine the crumbling 17th century memorials on the exterior of the Church — memorials to the great, but almost forgotten, Orthodox theologians, such as Balthasar Meisner and J. A. Quenstedt, who made Wittenberg the center of the Biblical and systematic Lutheranism of their day: what a responsibility this building imposes upon the theological visitor who will himself have to account one day to his Redeemer for his stewardship of God's mysteries!

And what a shock to find that in one of the Castle towers a Communist Youth organization now meets, and that a "Museum für Naturkunde und Völkerkunde" is now established — with a bilingual German-Russian plaque on the door — in still another section of the Schloss. Thus does the East German regime appropriate Luther: as a nationalistic hero and an opponent of "church authority"! But Luther survived more serious trials than this in his own day.

My afternoon in Wittenberg focused upon the Lutherhalle — the Luther museum and library — which house one of the most outstanding historical collections of material on Luther available anywhere in the world. While inquiring about a photostat of a MS that I had ordered months before in Strasbourg but had never received, I was told, by a French-speaking scholar in attendance (his name must remain anonymous for obvious reasons) that the document had indeed been sent, and its non-arrival displayed "the kind of freedom we experience here." "But," said I, leading him on, "I saw sign after sign in East Germany proclaiming 'Freiheit'." "Exactly," he replied, "and this is the only place you will find freedom here."

THE WARTBURG: CASTLE AND CHAMPAGNE

I had spent more time than intended in Wittenberg. Having purchased some scholarly volumes at the Lutherhalle and having bade farewell to the above-mentioned gentleman who said poignantly as I left, "Next time you come, bring us freedom," I retraced my route to Eisenach. My plan was to see the Wartburg — the Castle where Luther, driven into hiding by the Im-

THE WARTBURG CASTLE

perial ban, spent his days and nights translating the New Testament so that even a plowboy could read Christ's very words.

The shadows of evening were just coming on as I reached Eisenach, where Luther had attended a preparatory Latin school before entering the University of Erfurt. Poised on a hill outside Eisenach is that magnificent pile, the Wartburg. But how to reach it? After several false starts, I saw a young, college-age couple coming out of a movie theater, and asked directions. The boy spoke some English, and was visibly excited on learning that I was an American. So I invited the two to accompany me to the Castle. We arrived without difficulty, parked the car, and proceeded the last few hundred yards on foot. The moon had risen; the couple tuned their transistor radio to the U.S. Armed Forces radio station broadcasting from across the border, and, arm in arm, we "sang along" with the numbers being played. On reaching the Castle, the boy insisted that, after looking about, we go to its cafe-restaurant and share a bottle of champagne. Refusal was impossible; indeed, he even persuaded the waitress to allow us to occupy a table on the (then closed) patio overlooking the Castle parapets.

There the three of us sat and talked, and sipped Russian champagne (the boy apologized for it — and had every reason to do so! — but the Russian vintage was the only thing obtainable). The boy and girl were engaged; he was an engineering student at a Technische Hochschule, and both hoped that in the near future marriage would be possible for them. Yet both were pessimistic and discouraged about their personal future and about the future of their land. The boy had a taste of Western European life (he had lived with his father in the West, but had had the misfortune of returning to his mother's home in East Germany just before the DDR travel restrictions were imposed); having experienced freedom, he longed for it passionately. "You have no idea how bad it is here," they both told me; "Walter Ulbricht is nothing but a dictator."

My time was running out; midnight was fast approaching. The couple insisted on footing the bill and accompanying me as near to the checkpoint as possible. About a kilometer from the gate, I stopped the car. Before getting out, the student hugged me. It was with tears in our eyes that we expressed the hope of meeting again in a better day.

REFLECTIONS

On the long drive back to Strasbourg, many thoughts crossed my mind. God gave the Gospel to "the Jew first" — and as a result of rejecting it, he first drank the cup of God's wrath as well (Rom. 1:16; 2:8-10). Is Germany's sorry history in modern times in part at least the result of a similar rejection of special grace — as bestowed in Luther's Reform? If so, does Luther's Germany constitute a handwriting on the wall for our own nation — originally a refuge for those who wished to proclaim and live Biblical truth, now a refuge for those who would benefit from an astronomical standard of living?

And is "peaceful coexistence" really a moral option when so many of the world's people such as those I met in East Germany, are experiencing anything but daily "peace"? I am certainly no "American firster," but I seriously question the ethics of "live and let live" in our world. It appears to me that for the Christian at least, who has been set free by the blood of Christ and who knows, with Luther, what it means to be "a free Christian man," there should be every legitimate positive effort made to liberate the bodies and the souls of those whose life perspective has been so horribly attenuated by totalitarianism. "As He died to make men holy, let us die to make men free": not, we pray, through war, but through dying to ourselves in the active promotion of liberty on the earth. As Gwyn Thomas has well said: "We may sojourn briefly or long in some enchanted castle like the Wartburg, as Luther did, protected by the shield of a genial, friendly prince. Then we may play with the idea of withdrawal and peace. But the night will come when old, long-fingered dreams will tap at the windows. A door will open on the road we have to go, toward some climactic affirmation of faith which will end with Luther's words: 'Here I stand. Amen.' "

To utter these words from the heart is to enter Luther country indeed.

V
LUTHER AND THE MISSIONARY CHALLENGE

On October 31, 1967, Christendom celebrated the 450th anniversary of an event that decisively altered the religious climate of the Western world: Luther's posting of the Ninety-Five Theses on the Castle Church door at Wittenberg. The original door has long since disappeared, but it has been appropriately replaced by a monumental door on which the text of the Theses has been permanently engraved. Luther's message is indeed permanently engraved on the history of the world, and his recovery of the Gospel stands behind evangelical proclamation from that day to this. But was his "Copernican revolution in theology" (as Philip Watson has felicitously termed it) more than an evangelical monument? Was it also an evangelical *movement?* A current joke has to do with a new Martin Luther doll: you wind it up and it just "stands there!" Did Luther just stand there — at Wittenberg, at Leipzig, at Worms, at Marburg — or did he move dynamically with a sense of mission to the lost?

The Stereotype of an Unconcerned Luther

The great Protestant missionary scholar Gustav Warneck of Halle regarded the Reformation in general and Luther in particular as anything but missionary-minded, and Warneck's negative evaluation has had much influence on lesser writers. Wrote Warneck in the standard *New Schaff-Herzog Encyclopedia of Religious Knowledge* (based on the great Herzog and Hauck *Realencyklopaedie*): "The comprehension of a continuous missionary duty of the Church was limited among the Reformers and their successors by a narrow-minded dogmatism combined with a lack of historical sense. They knew of the great missions of the past, but according to their ideas the apostles had already gone forth to the whole world and they and their disciples had essentially accomplished the missionary task. Christianity, therefore, had already proved its universal vocation as a world religion." Elsewhere, Warneck stated that in Luther one misses not only "missionary activity" but also the very "idea of missions," and he refers to the reformer as hardly "a man of missions in our sense of the word."

To which Luther scholar Werner Elert replied sarcastically in his *Structure of Lutheranism:* "Poor Luther! Instead of founding a missionary society, accompanying Cortez to Mexico, or at least assuring for himself a professorship of missionary science, he devoted himself, of all things, to the reformation of the church! ... How could Luther, who expounded the Psalms, the Prophets, and Paul, have overlooked or doubted the universal purpose of the mission of Christ and of His Gospel?" A good question — and one that gains even greater force when one considers the extent of missionary activity carried on by the church bearing Luther's name during the two centuries immediately following his split with Rome. Charles Porterfield Krauth nicely tabulated the record in his important work, *The Conservative Reformation and Its Theology*:

> Nor has the Lutheran Church been satisfied with meeting the wants of her own children. She has been, and is a Church of Missions. In 1559, Gustavus Vasa, of Sweden, founded a mission among the Laplanders, which was continued with renewed earnestness by Gustavus Adolphus, Denmark also aiding. Thomas von Westen (died 1727) was the apostle of this mission. Heyling, of Lübeck, without any aid, labored as a missionary in Abyssinia (1635), and others, of the circle of his friends, engaged in the same cause in various parts of the East. Frederick IV, of Denmark, established the East India mission at Tranquebar (1706), for which Francke furnished him two devoted laborers, Plützschau and Ziegenbalg, the latter of whom translated the New Testament into Tamil (1715). The labors of this mission were also extended to the English possessions. From the orphan-house at Halle went forth a succession of missionaries, among whom Schwartz (died 1798) is pre-eminent. An institution for the conversion of the Jews was established at Halle, in 1728. Egede of Norway (died 1758) commenced his labors in Greenland, in 1721. In 1736, he returned, and established in Copenhagen a mission seminary.

But could it not be argued that much of this Lutheran missionary zeal stemmed not from Luther himself, but from the influence of post-Reformation Pietism? Perhaps — but only if one neglects to examine Luther's own views on the subject of missions. In this area of Luther's thought, as in so many others, the reformer has suffered greatly from his 18th and 19th century interpreters, who have often seriously misunderstood and misrepresented his actual beliefs. Indeed, the great Luther research movement of the present century, deriving largely from the work of Karl Holl, has revolutionized our understanding of the reformer precisely because it has insisted on letting him speak for himself.

LUTHER ON MISSIONS

Two deadly misconceptions concerning Luther's missionary stance need to be removed at the outset. It has been held that Luther's views lie at the root of a famous (better, infamous) post-Reformation judgment of the Wittenberg theological faculty as to the scope of the Great Commission. When Count Truchsess posed this question to the faculty, its members issued a document declaring that the command to go into all the world was only a *personale privilegium* of the apostles, and had already been fulfilled; were this not so, the faculty reasoned, the duty of becoming a missionary evangelist would fall to every Christian — an absurd conclusion! World evangelism would violate the creative orders (*Schöpfungsordnungen*) by which God gives each man a stable place in society, sets rulers over their subjects, and requires a definite and limited call for ministerial service. Thus, the argument goes, Luther himself held that the world had already been totally evangelized, and maintained that since all church workers must be "duly called" (*rite vocati*), and the heathen obviously are not going to call Christian evangelists to serve them, missionary work is unjustifiable in principle.

To attribute such views to Luther is, however, to fly directly in the face of the evidence. In the first place, as Elert notes, "the idea of many later theologians — that the church of the present time is no longer obligated to preach among the heathen, because the apostles have already reached all — is totally foreign to Luther, just as it is to Melanchthon." Indeed, Luther specifically says of the "islands" brought to light during the Renaissance age of discovery that they are "heathen and no one has preached to them" (*Weimarer Ausgabe,* 23, 533, 10; etc.). As to the second charge against Luther, the Reformer himself asserts that when the Christian is at a place "where there are no Christians, there he needs no other call than that he is a Christian who is inwardly called and anointed by God. There it is his obligation to preach to the erring heathen and non-Christians, and to teach the Gospel as a duty of Christian love, even though no one calls him to do this" (*WA,* 11, 412, 11ff.).

For Luther, the proclamation of the Gospel is the Christian's highest privilege, and he should begin by exercising it in the normal situations of life. In a sermon he preached in his own home in 1533, he said: "The noblest and greatest work and the most important service we can perform for God on earth is bringing other people, and especially those who are entrusted to us, to the knowledge of God by the holy Gospel" (*WA*, 53, 415). It was Luther's conviction that missionary work ideally proceeds from the home base. True, as a child of his time, he held the common 16th century view that Christian "home bases" were more widely distributed in the world than was actually the case, but he certainly did not limit his vision to "home missions." Rather, his approach has strong parallels with the widely held view of 20th century evangelicals that the person who does not witness at home will not witness abroad, and that the individual who wants to go to the foreign field to escape the responsibility of living a life of Christian witness at home is the worst kind of missionary candidate.

If we doubt that Luther had a burden for the "foreign field," what will we do with such express words as these from his pen? "The very best of all works is that the heathen have been led from idolatry to the knowledge of God" (*WA*, 47, 466; sermon of Sept. 25, 1538, on Matt. 23:15). "In these New Testament times there is always a lack of Christians; there never are enough of them. Therefore we must not stop inviting guests to partake of this Paschal Lamb. We must keep on preaching. We must also go to those to whom Christ has hitherto not been proclaimed. We must teach the people who have not known Christ, so that they, too, may be brought to the spiritual kingdom of Christ" (*WA*, 16, 215f.).

Luther considered it axiomatic that the salvation of men everywhere depended squarely on the universal proclamation of the Gospel to them. In this, as in his central doctrine of justification by grace through faith, Luther's conscience was captive to the Pauline message.

> If all the heathen are to praise God, He must first have been made their God. If He is to be their God, they must know Him and believe on Him and let go of all idolatry. For man cannot praise God with idolatrous lips and an unbelieving heart. If they are to believe, they must first hear His Word and thus receive the Holy Spirit, who purifies and enlightens their heart by faith. For one cannot come to faith or receive the Holy Spirit before one has heard the Word, as Paul says (Rom. 10:14): "How shall they

believe in Him of whom they have not heard?"
(Gal. 3:2): You have received the Spirit by the
preaching of faith. If they are to hear His
Word, preachers who proclaim the Word of God
to them must be sent to them (*WA* 31 I, 228f.).

Not only in preaching and teaching, but also in hymnody
Luther expressed his profound missionary vision. The composer
of "A Mighty Fortress Is Our God," which so magnificently conveys the doctrinal heart of the Reformation, composed a mission
hymn that could be regarded as its evangelistic counterpart.
Luther wrote the hymn in 1524, basing it on Psalm 67. Here is
the Psalm, followed by the first stanza of Luther's rendition:

God be merciful unto us, and bless us; and
cause His face to shine upon us.

That Thy way may be known upon earth,
Thy saving health among all nations.

Let the people praise Thee, O God; let all
the people praise Thee.

O let the nations be glad and sing for joy:
for Thou shalt judge the people righteously, and
govern the nations upon earth.

Let the people praise Thee, O God; let all
the people praise Thee.

Then shall the earth yield her increase;
and God, even our own God, shall bless us.

God shall bless us; and all the ends of the
earth shall fear Him.

May God bestow on us His grace,
With blessings rich provide us,
And may the brightness of His face
To life eternal guide us
That we His saving health may know,
His gracious will and pleasure,
And also to the heathen show
Christ's riches without measure
And unto God convert them.

LUTHER'S MISSIONARY DYNAMIC

As Luther scholars such as Reu have shown, Luther considered Holy Scripture as the "formal principle" of all true theology: the fully authoritative, inerrant Word of God to man. For this reason he devoted tireless energy to translating the Bible into the German vernacular, so "any plowboy could hear Christ's word"; and for this reason he searched the Scriptures for God's missionary message. Thus Luther drew from Abraham's faith-directed journeys an important lesson concerning God's sovereign guidance in the spread of His Gospel.

> God is wont to deal so with His own that He does not let them stay long at one place. He rushes them here and there, not merely for their own sakes, so that their faith be tested, but also for the benefit of other people. For Abraham could, of course, not remain silent. Nor was it fitting that he should not preach to the people about the grace of God. God drove him into Egypt by hunger that he might do some good there too and enlighten some with the true knowledge of God. This he no doubt did, for it is impossible for one to associate with people without revealing what serves their soul's salvation (*WA*, 24, 261).

How little such a passage as this conforms to the stereotype of a Luther who expected Christians to remain statically where they were — in the fixed orders of life — witnessing solely to those locked into the same life-structures with them!

Similarly, Luther draws a powerful missionary lesson from the story of Joseph. As Joseph in Egypt told his brothers to hurry back to their father Jacob with the good news of God's providence, so God through Christ (whom Joseph typified) wants us to tell others of His grace: "After we have learned to know God in His Son and have received the forgiveness of sins and the Holy Spirit, who endues hearts with joy and with the peace of soul by which we look with contempt on sin and death, what remains to be done? Go, and do not be silent. You are not the only one to be saved; a multitude of others remain who must be preserved from destruction" (*WA*, 44, 612).

What was the source of Luther's missionary dynamic, as revealed in these scriptural applications? Professor George Forell has well termed it "faith active in love." For Luther, the fact that God has saved us freely in Christ, in spite of our unworthiness, means that we are freed from the bondage and anxiety of our sins to serve our fellow men with self-giving love. Instead of attempting to placate God through monastic piety or other supposed methods of self-salvation, we will listen to God, who, "having no need for our work and benefactions for Himself, bids us to do for our neighbor what we would do for God" (*WA*, 17, 98; cf. Ziemke's *Love for the Neighbor in Luther's Theology*). And what, above all, ought we to do for our neighbors on this sin-sick globe? Proclaim to them the eternal riches of Christ!

> Nothing but faith is needed to be saved, to give God the honor due Him and to accept Him as my God, confessing that He is just, true, and merciful. Such faith sets us free from sin and all evil. If I have thus given God His due, I live the rest of my life for the benefit of my neighbor, to serve and help him. The greatest work that follows from faith is that with my mouth I confess Christ, sealing that confession with my blood and, if it is so to be, laying down my life for it. Not that God needs this work. But I am to do it that my faith may thereby be proved and known, that others may likewise be brought to believe. Then other works follow; they must all be directed toward serving my neighbor (*WA*, 12, 288). . . . . .
>
> The Lord wants to say: You have received enough from Me — peace and joy and everything you ought to have; personally you need no more. Therefore work now, look at what I have done, and imitate it. My Father has sent Me into the world for your sake alone, in order to help you, not to benefit Myself. This I have done; I have died for you and have given you all I am and have. Therefore you should think and act in like manner. Henceforth you should spend your lives serving and helping everyone; otherwise you would have nothing to do on earth, for through faith you have enough of everything. Therefore I send you into the world as My Father has sent Me, that is, that every Christian may instruct and teach his fellow man also to come to Christ (*WA*, 12, 521).

Missions, in sum, is the fruit of the Gospel. Luther sees the active declaration of God's saving message as a natural concomitant of the Christian life. Specifically, missionary effort follows dynamically from (1) the personal relationship with Christ, (2) the presence of the Holy Spirit in the believing heart, and (3) the powerful working of God's Word, which never returns void. In his exposition of John 14:12-14 (1537), Luther describes the connection between the saving experience and the proclamation of the Gospel to others:

> When a Christian begins to know Christ as His Lord and Savior, who has redeemed him from death, and is brought into His dominion and heritage, his heart is thoroughly permeated by God; then he would like to help everybody attain this blessedness. For he has no greater joy than the treasured knowledge of Christ. So he begins to teach and exhort others, confesses and commends his blessedness before everybody, and sighs and prays that they, too, may come to this grace. He has a restless spirit while enjoying rest supreme, that is, God's grace and peace. Therefore he cannot be quiet or idle but is forever struggling and striving with all his powers, as one living only to spread God's honor and praise farther among men, to cause others also to receive this spirit of grace and through it also to help him pray (*WA*, 45, 540).

Luther's comments on the "fruits of the Spirit" in Gal. 5:22 (1531) include his affirmation that joy in spreading the Gospel in one of the Spirit's benefits: "The godly rejoice when the Gospel is widely spread, many come to faith, and Christ's kingdom is increased in this way" (*WA*, 40 II, 118). In a letter of March, 1522, Luther stresses the vital connecton between missionary proclamation and the power of God's Word — in the threefold sense of Christ, His Gospel, and the Scripture that conveys it: "This noble Word brings with it a great hunger and an insatiable thirst, so that we could not be satisfied even though many thousands of people believe on it; we wish that no one should be without it. This thirst ever strives for more and does not rest; it moves us to speak, as David says: 'I believe, therefore have I spoken' (Ps. 116:10). And we have (says St. Paul, II Cor. 4:13) 'the same spirit of faith . . . we also believe and therefore speak' "

(*WA*, 10 II, 54). Here we have Luther's philosophy of missions, distilled in six scriptural words: "I believed, therefore have I spoken."

LESSONS FROM LUTHER

Not only does Luther have a superlative missionary vision; he has vital lessons for us who live in a world of jet age, mass communications evangelism methods. Two paramount lessons can be drawn from Luther's understanding of the missionary task. Whatever our denominational or confessional connections, we should listen closely to his Scriptural insights.

First, the focus of missions must be, *not sociology but theology — not man in his sin, but God and His grace.* When Luther's critics condemn him for not setting forth specific missionary methods and techniques, they simply display their own obtuseness. "This reproach," says Elert with full justice, "belongs in the technical high schools, where the science of business is taught"; and in the spirit of Luther he adds: "Only from the dynamic of the Gospel itself can the 'idea of missions,' which should be evangelical, get its obligating power, not from reflecting on this or that kind of people." Today we have become preoccupied with methods and techniques of mission, to the point where the gravitational center of the missionary thrust has perceptibly shifted from God to man. Perhaps we are in need of a "Copernican revolution" in missions, based on Luther's insights, which will restore the proper center to evangelistic proclamation, even as Luther's original message restored a Christocentric perspective to theology. In an address at Trinity Evangelical Divinity School, C. Stacey Woods of the International Fellowship of Evangelical Students made much the same point: evangelicals today are not having the missionary impact that the last generation did, in spite of (or perhaps because of) their sociological techniques; the answer is a return to the Word as the source of all true missionary dynamic.

Second, we can learn from Luther that in the final analysis the motive for missions must be, *not legalism but love.* "God lets us live here on earth in order that we may lead other people to believe, doing for them what He has done for us" (*WA*, 12, 267). We love the lost because God in Christ loved us when we were lost. Missions follows the heart recognition that Christ has given Himself for us. Legal motivations are superfluous, for the good tree (as Luther was fond of saying) bears good fruit; you don't have to waggle your finger and instruct it! Missionary activity, therefore, is not something to be legalistically schematized into "home" and "foreign" missions (with greater "merit" generally attaching to the latter); as the great 19th century Lutheran missions developer Wilhelm Loehe said, in Luther's spirit, "Missions is nothing but the one church of God in its motion."

For Luther, the missionary enterprise is the outgrowth of love — no more, no less; and he characteristically employed two of the most fundamental Biblical symbols of love, water and fire, in setting forth his dynamic vision of Christian proclamation to a world desperately needing an eternal Word of love. When the Gospel message is proclaimed, it is "as if one threw a stone into the water; the stone causes ripples, circles, and streams round about it; and the ripples always roll them farther and farther; one drives the other until they come to the shore. Although the water becomes calm in the center, the ripples do not rest but keep on flowing" (*WA*, 10 III, 140, 6ff.). "Christians should also bring forth much fruit among all the heathen by means of the Word, should convert and save many by eating about themselves like a fire that burns amid dry wood or straw; thus the fire of the Holy Spirit should consume the heathen according to the flesh and make room everywhere for the Gospel and the kingdom of Christ" (*WA*, 23, 645, 30). May we in our day become so consumed by the fire of Christ's love that we spend our lives conveying living water to all who thirst for the "pure river of life, clear as crystal, that proceedeth out of the throne of God and of the Lamb."

LIST OF ILLUSTRATIONS

INDEX OF PERSONS